Trauma: Healing the Hidden , ... ~p~.. uic uuor to an emerging condition which all Americans need to understand and respect.

Physical, emotional and mental trauma have touched every one of us to some degree. Our dilemma has continued to be how each of us confronts this challenge---whether the condition be our own or a loved one's.

Doctor Bernstein has taken a complex and potentially deadly condition, and simplified it as best as humanly possible. Do not mistake simplification for lack of depth, however. Like me, the reader will finish (this book) with the tools and confidence that trauma can be healed.

Former US Navy SEAL
Rear Admiral Ray Smith
USN Retired

I found *Trauma: Healing the Hidden Epidemic* to be an exemplary work in understanding the connections between mind, body, and spirit when faced with enormous hardship, suffering, and pain.

Bernstein's personal and professional accounts provide an open window into how traumatic injuries (physical, emotional, and psychological) manifest and progress over time if not treated early.

Bernstein's warning about long-term residual and consequences of untreated trauma should be in the forefront of education and training to our Service Members, veterans and their families.

This book is a welcome addition to the literature on traumatology, crisis-intervention, stress-management, and psychological and spiritual health during an era of terrorism, war, and economic challenges in the U.S.

Colonel David D. Rabb, LICSW, ACSW
United States Army Reserve, Combat Stress Control
OIF/OEF War Veteran

"A terrific read!! *Trauma: Healing the Hidden Epidemic* is written in a way that makes a complex subject easy to understand. I particularly liked the passages about the mind-body interaction.

I believe that Dr. Bernstein would be valuable as an adviser / consultant to the VA on TBI / PTSD.

Trauma should be on the reading list at V.A. clinics."

General Richard D. Hearney, Retired
Former Assistant Commandant, Marine Corps

"Just like healing any wound, trauma can and should be treated. In *Trauma: Healing the Hidden Epidemic,* it is clear that what some believe as permanent damage can be reversed.

Bernstein explores treating trauma; military experience can build a man, war will tear a man apart, and Bernstein guides us through rebuilding that man.

This rebuilding is the mission, and it is clear, if allowed the proper treatment, the body will heal itself. We, as a community, need to support those who have these wounds; support the recovery to help their body heal, from the inside out. Allowing them and their loved ones to fully participate in life again."

Elece Hempel
Executive Director
Petaluma People Services Center

"Trauma: Healing the Hidden Epidemic, by Dr. Peter Bernstein, provides a clear and uncomplicated understanding of the nature and treatment of trauma for all readers, lay people and professionals alike.

All the information is there, nothing is too confusing or esoteric, you don't have to look terms up in the dictionary to know what's going on. Peter's key contribution to the field of trauma treatment is that he has brought the body into psychotherapy.

By combining principles of classic psychotherapy with myofascial release, creating RMFR, Peter offers a comprehensive and effective new approach to the trauma treatment field.

Lay people usually feel left out of in-depth discussions of trauma because of unfamiliar language and theories. Not so with this book. Peter de-mystifies and shares his extensive knowledge of PTSD – what it is and how to treat it – in language everyone can understand."

Armando Maliano
Master addiction specialist for 50 years
Former Clinical Director of the Family Therapy Institute of Marin
Former Clinical Director and President of the Board of Center Point
Inc., Drug & Alcohol Treatment Programs

This book should meet a real need - to inform "the man/woman on the street" of the signs and effects of trauma. Surely, it will encourage readers to seek help they may not have known they needed.

I especially appreciated (the) clear explanation of what determines the traumatic nature of an event. This, clearly written in a lay-person's language, is but one illustration of the well-defined voice of the manuscript.

I pray this tool will reach its intended audience and that many who suffer from trauma will find courage to seek help.

Joy Gage,
Popular Christian Author
Mentor, Christian Writer's Guild

TRAUMA:
Healing the Hidden Epidemic

By Peter Bernstein, Ph.D.

CONTENTS

To the Reader   i

1   Understanding Trauma   1

2   Emotional Blueprints and Developmental Trauma   11

3   Trauma and Your Body   21

4   Finding a Solution   31

5   Taking It to the Next Level   39

6   Seeking Treatment   51

7   A Note to Veterans and Their Loved Ones   67

8   Danger Signals and Trauma First Aid   81

9   Crises and Hard Times   95

10   The Spirituality of Healing   107

Acknowledgments   115

Bibliography   119

About Dr. Bernstein   121

DEDICATION

I dedicate this book to our fallen heroes—America's military service members who have made the ultimate sacrifice of their lives in recent conflicts around the world—and their families. I also dedicate this work to our returning warriors who bear physical and hidden emotional wounds of war. My heart's desire is that my message will reach them, providing encouragement, relief from pain, healing, and hope for a better life.

The efforts of every one of us will be necessary to counter the horrors of combat and its traumatizing impact on our service members and their families. I sincerely hope that our communities will come together to support these courageous men and women as they face a new battlefield: reintegration and adjustment to life back home. Veterans, active duty personnel, and their families all deserve our acknowledgement and assistance—not only in words, but in actions.

Bless our heroes; I am grateful. May we all be grateful.

TO THE READER

What is trauma? Why do its effects last far beyond the event or events that caused it? Why are our human reactions to it so debilitating? Most importantly, how can we help someone heal the deep wounds that it can leave in its wake? These are the questions I've been investigating for over forty years, and I believe I have found some answers.

The unique approach to healing the effects of trauma revealed in this book is considered radical by some in the psychological field, and it may be—but it works. Drugs and talk therapy may be necessary tools on the road to restoring health to a trauma victim, but they are not enough to truly heal—in mind, body, and spirit—the unconscious wounds left by traumatic experiences.

What constitutes a traumatic experience? We often think of it as a harrowing, near-death experience that causes severe emotional shock, and sometimes it is. But, that is only one type of trauma; in the world of psychology, we call it "shock" trauma. Many other types of trauma are described in this book. Misunderstandings about what causes trauma, what makes an experience traumatic, and what heals the wounds that can linger decades after the initial event or experience compelled me to create this primer. I wrote it to help the average person better understand trauma and what steps can be taken to heal from its devastating effects.

It isn't only survivors of disaster or military service members and their families who suffer (and they do suffer, in record numbers); it's people of all ages, from all walks of life, who have experienced the unexpected in dramatic and disturbing ways. They may not even remember the circumstances of the initial traumatic experience, but the detrimental impact on their lives is unmistakable. It happens to children as they are growing up, described as *developmental* trauma. It happens to adults who suffer *emotional* trauma. Economic uncertainty or financial calamity, or the loss of a home, job, business, or life's savings in a destabilized economy can aggravate symptoms of emotional or developmental trauma incurred years earlier. In addition, a subsequent situation or event can compound the original injury. Even those who care for trauma victims can suffer something we call *secondary* trauma. All of these types of trauma, left untreated, lead to the same end: a much compromised life that is frequently stressful, often painful, and sometimes unbearable.

There is help for those courageous enough to ask for it. Healing is possible. We have witnessed such healing time and again at the Bernstein Institute for Trauma Treatment in Petaluma, California. However, only by addressing the wounds lodged deep in our subconscious mind and, quite literally, in our bodies can true healing begin. The process of discovering and developing a method of healing at this profound level is described in this book.

Have the undesirable effects of trauma in this country reached epidemic proportions? We believe so; we see the suffering at the institute on a daily basis. As the effects of trauma become more clearly understood, we begin to see its damage on a much larger scale. In the past ten years, we have seen not only an enormous surge in the number of military veterans affected by trauma but also an increase in patients who did not previously recognize their symptoms as having resulted from trauma. The good news is that relief can be found and healing is possible.

For victims of trauma who may be reading this, know that it's not unusual to feel ashamed of your past, even if the darkest moments in your life were not your fault. You may not want to admit to your friends or even to yourself that you are unable to function normally, that you were abused, that most areas of your life are dysfunctional, or that you have explosive relationships.

Regardless of the circumstances, you may seek to hide the parts of your life that are not perfect. You may feel shame in admitting that you have been a victim of your surroundings, or a victim of any sort.

It is the nature of humanity, particularly in our success-obsessed culture, to want to keep these facts to ourselves, and even *from* ourselves. We may have learned that it is improper to discuss such events. We may fear judgment for our inadequacies and feel like failures if we cannot demonstrate total control. The prospect of transparently sharing the horrors we have experienced may be overwhelming. We are programmed to maintain the illusion of perfection. Yet maintaining this illusion of perfection, or, at the very least, the illusion of *control*, has cost many victims of trauma their lives. Don't let that person be you or your loved one. Read this book. Seek solutions. You do not have to live with the effects of untreated trauma, and you do not have to die or medicate yourself to escape them.

I know these things not only because I have many years of academic training and experience as a therapist working with victims of trauma; I know because I have experienced the damaging effects of trauma in a violent childhood and while living on the edge of a criminal early adulthood. I share some of my story in this book to help readers better understand their own stories.

It has been a long journey from the scared little boy I once was to the man I am now. Along the way, I have found that healing from trauma is possible, if one is willing to do the work involved. The first step toward this healing is to begin to understand trauma and its effects on one's mind, body, and spirit. I hope this book helps victims of trauma and their loved ones take that first step, and I pray it offers them hope and courage in taking the steps that follow.

CHAPTER 1

Understanding Trauma

Trauma does not discriminate. It happens to all kinds of people under many different circumstances. Regardless, the repercussions are clear: Life becomes increasingly difficult, chaotic, and unmanageable. Unexpected and painfully unwelcome, the symptoms of trauma reveal themselves—sometimes slowly, sometimes suddenly—as nightmares, confusion, relentless anxiety, sleeplessness or fatigue. Although this intruder wears many disguises, the fallout of traumatic experience is the same: We are wounded—physically, mentally, and emotionally.

Physiologically, when we experience a traumatic event, or a series of traumatic events, our innate stress response is triggered. The brain signals the body to release a flood of hormones and neurochemicals, instantaneously launching us into a hyper-alert state and causing muscle contractions, acute alertness, and concentrated attention on our immediate environment. This is obviously a valuable survival mechanism; however, unlike with other creatures in the animal kingdom, this involuntary stress response in humans can be interrupted, the "energy" of the response being stored, in a sense, by the influence of our rational brain. (See chapter 3 for more detail.) The biological response is left unresolved, literally lodged in our bodies, our minds, and our emotional reactions. We are left incapable of functioning the way we might have before the effects of trauma invaded our lives. It changes us emotionally and physically in ways that can render us ill-equipped to deal with life's difficulties. It distorts the way we view the world, the people in it, and ourselves. Years of confusion, pain, suffering, and loneliness can result, even if people who care for us surround us. Trauma is not just a snapshot in time. It can warp every moment that follows it.

It can affect our relationships with our children, our spouses, or our parents. We may struggle with self-esteem, never feeling quite good enough. Or we might battle even more destructive demons, such as depression or addiction, unable to free ourselves from them no matter how hard we try. We may wonder why life is so inherently challenging for us. If that is the case, it is likely that the aftermath of trauma is at work in our lives.

At the Bernstein Institute for Integrative Psychotherapy & Trauma Treatment, we specialize in addressing trauma and post-traumatic stress disorder of many origins. We've had a long-standing commitment to soldiers and military families in need, and their numbers have multiplied drastically over the past four decades. However, we see all kinds of trauma victims in addition to veterans—victims of car accidents and natural disasters, physically abused spouses, survivors of criminal acts, adults who suffered abusive childhoods, and many victims who are unaware of what incident or situation causes them to feel such desperation. They often feel they cannot go on living with their current relentless level of anxiety, sleeplessness, pain, or numerous other symptoms any longer.

It is disturbing to see the mounting wave of trauma victims coming through our doors, a larger wave than I've seen in forty years of practice. In addition to its effect on afflicted military service members and their families, the swell of this pandemic seems to have reached many thousands of Americans who have lost businesses, jobs, homes, and health in the fallout of a severely strained economy. The effect of trauma experienced earlier in their lives is compounded by the increasing stress of meeting current everyday needs. They reach a breaking point, and their trauma symptoms—insomnia, anxiety, and a host of other distortions and discomforts—proliferate and intensify.

Thankfully, we are able to help many of those who are suffering by focusing on a solution that treats the whole person—body, mind, and spirit.

Recovery Is Possible

The emotional and physical damage caused by the invasion of trauma can be healed. We can be restored to the capable people we were meant to be, coping with our current reality instead of being haunted by a reality long since gone.

A key component in healing the effects of trauma and putting our lives back together is the knowledge that, in our experience, talk therapy alone is seldom enough. (Such therapy is often called cognitive behavioral therapy, or CBT.) Though it can be a valuable starting place, this common approach to healing the damage done by trauma is seldom adequate for addressing the wounds that remain stored deep within us, concealed in our cells. We have found that the best results come when we focus on healing the mind *and* body.

If we are to heal from these injuries—physical, emotional, and psychological—we must acknowledge the changes that have taken place in our bodies (which may feel as if they are betraying us), as well as in our psyches, where a distortion of our emotional lives and our thinking has taken place.

As we begin to understand how and why trauma intrudes on our lives, we must consider all aspects of our injuries. As I have discovered over years of treating trauma victims (and seeking help for myself), it takes more than merely talking about the effects of trauma to escape the devastation of this mysterious and malicious invader.

Human beings respond to trauma in a very sophisticated and complex way. As noted above, reactions to trauma are physical (biological), emotional, and psychological. All of these reactions are intertwined and interrelated. The sequence of events that causes a person to become traumatized, however, is fairly straightforward.

First, a traumatic incident occurs (or even several traumatic incidents). Next, our brain triggers a biological response to that event. If that biological process is unable to reach completion, if we are unable to fully discharge the "energy" created by such an event, we become traumatized. We might subsequently develop physiological and psychological symptoms and behaviors that significantly interfere with our life and the lives of those around us. At this stage, we would be—clinically speaking—*traumatized*.

Trauma, whether physical or emotional, is synonymous with damage. In the world of psychology, trauma is an emotional injury, wound, or state of shock that results from a single event or series of events. Violence or physical trauma often accompanies emotional trauma. Sometimes, it does not. Any event outside the realm of normal human experience that could be universally acknowledged as distressing, however, is generally described as trauma. Certain events, such as those listed here, are almost always traumatic:

- Serious illness, injury, accident, or disability
- Death of a loved one
- Divorce or loss of a significant relationship
- Child abuse or neglect
- Incest, rape, domestic abuse, or violence
- Criminal violence or assault

- Military combat, law enforcement, fire-fighting, and rescue experiences
- The witnessing of horrific events
- Natural disasters, terrorist attacks

These experiences often leave serious emotional wounds, regardless of the victim's age, situation, individual characteristics, or personality. Some situations that are significantly less dramatic can be just as traumatic as those listed above. The traumatic nature of an event or series of ongoing events is determined by whether the event was expected, whether we felt prepared for the event, and ultimately, our reaction to that event. Our emotional and physical *reaction* to that event is what causes trauma. This means that lesser events can be just as damaging and the symptoms equally invasive:

- Surgery
- Illness
- Relocation, moving
- Financial distress
- Bullying
- Job loss

Types of Trauma

In the medical world, the word trauma usually describes physical damage that can be seen or detected with medical technology. It may be visible or could leave a scar. The evidence of the pain associated with the event is there on the surface, and we can point to it and say, "This happened to me, and it's real." When a person sustains a physical injury, it is usually treated with a sense of urgency, and all the necessary measures are taken to ensure a complete and timely recovery. Eventually, most victims of this type of trauma can pull the bandage away and see that the physical damage has healed. Their health has been restored.

The most common form of trauma, however, goes above and beyond physical wounds. Often, its victims don't even remember when or how it happened. This is called *emotional trauma*, the invisible wound, and it affects almost every human on earth at some point in his or her life. A person could be dealing with the effects of emotional trauma now without even knowing it. The source of trauma may be unclear, yet the scars it leaves behind can be very difficult to hide. Many people feel the effects of their emotional wounds every day, even though they may have no idea what caused them.

Emotional traumas are as real as physical traumas, and every bit as damaging. They need to be treated quickly and effectively to reduce the potential for painful, long-term symptoms. Because there may not be any visible or detectable evidence that an emotionally damaging event has taken place, this type of trauma often remains untreated.

Developmental trauma is a traumatic event or series of events that occurs during a person's childhood or "developmental" years. While a child's physical body is growing and maturing, his or her psyche is developing as well. Trauma interrupts this growth and changes the direction of development. Abuse (physical or sexual), neglect, abandonment, divorce, marital and familial conflict, rejection, illness, accidents, medical procedures, relocations, and countless other experiences can be traumatizing for a child. A parent or caregiver may not be aware that a traumatic event has taken place or how the child has been affected by it. He or she may have caused harm without even realizing it. These wounds can drastically alter one's future. (Chapter 2, "Emotional Blueprints and Developmental Trauma," examines emotional and developmental trauma in more detail. Suggestions for parents and caregivers are included in chapter 6, "Seeking Treatment, and chapter 9, Crises and Hard Times.")

Shock trauma describes isolated events or a limited series of events that are well outside the range of what most would consider normal human experience. Unlike developmental trauma, which occurs over time during the formative years of a person's life, shock trauma happens quickly, sometimes in a single moment. These shocking moments can be traumatic at any point in life and are usually experienced as short, singular events that send our nervous systems into overdrive, after which trauma symptoms begin their relentless intrusion. Most of us are unable to reprogram our nervous systems without experienced assistance.

Again, we may not be able to explain *why* we were traumatized by episodes in our lives; we might even feel embarrassed that certain events affected us to such an extent. However, no amount of embarrassment or minimizing of our symptoms will change the fact that past experiences are hindering our ability to function well in our present lives. Regardless of the nature of the traumatizing experience, the symptoms of trauma are very real and should be taken seriously.

Signs of Trauma

People suffering from emotional trauma often experience similar symptoms even if their backgrounds and circumstances are significantly different. Symptoms of emotional trauma are so common that many symptoms are downplayed or outright ignored. We may not realize that our issues, behaviors, and even health problems could be indications of past emotional trauma.

Such symptoms may include the following:

- Depression
- Sleep disturbances, nightmares, insomnia

- Sexual dysfunction or promiscuity
- Chronic pain
- Indigestion
- Attention deficit hyperactivity disorder (ADHD)
- Mood swings
- Low energy, chronic fatigue
- Inability to maintain healthy relationships
- Low self-esteem, lack of confidence
- Codependent or enabling relationships

Countless people experience one or more of the above at some point in their life, not knowing that these symptoms might be connected to a much bigger (and treatable) emotional issue. Other signs of trauma are more dramatic, such as eating disorders, preoccupation with or thoughts of death, or chronic substance abuse.

Symptoms of trauma appear in examples from our experience throughout this book. These are not technically rendered "case" histories; rather, they are simple stories of trauma patients and their families that illustrate an array of symptoms and correlated events in which readers might see themselves or someone they love. Many of the patients described in this book have experienced extraordinary healing.

Progressive Stages of Trauma

Early trauma symptoms may go unnoticed, tending to be milder and less disruptive to our lives. They are often disregarded as "just brief episodes." Immediately after an initial traumatic incident, we may experience difficulty sleeping, hyperactivity, and an inability to focus. Moodiness, inability to deal with stress, and even nightmares are also common responses. These symptoms may not have an adverse effect right away, but, over time, they can seriously affect our health and relationships. Difficulty sleeping, for instance, can diminish physical immunity as well as mental health. In an already challenging world, it can be debilitating to deal with the stress of trauma. Nevertheless, a person could live with these symptoms for a while without reaching a crisis point. Unfortunately, these symptoms usually get worse over time.

Intermediate-stage reactions include more severe, abnormal behaviors and symptoms. Forgetfulness, the inability to make commitments or to love or bond with others, drastically increased or decreased sexual activity and desire, fear of dying or going crazy, avoidance behavior, panic attacks, and anxiety are classic symptoms of mid-stage trauma. While these behaviors can be quite disruptive in a person's life, they are often ignored. They can be mistakenly attributed to personality, illness, or chemical imbalances. Even medical doctors falsely diagnose these symptoms. While other conditions can cause some of these reactions, people experiencing these symptoms are often responding to a traumatic event.

In the latest stages of unresolved trauma, symptoms become increasingly debilitating. Late-stage trauma symptoms can significantly interfere with our ability to function in a productive way. These behaviors might include chronic depression, feelings of isolation, lack of interest in life, feelings of helplessness, excessive shyness, and diminished emotional responses. Trauma can also lead to physiological symptoms such as immune deficiencies and endocrine problems, headaches, neck and back pain, asthma, digestive issues, PMS, and chronic fatigue, just to name a few. Ultimately, hopelessness and suicidal thoughts can set in; these are, without a doubt, the most dangerous of all trauma symptoms.

It is important to remember that late-stage trauma symptoms don't *replace* earlier symptoms. Instead, the symptoms are layered on top of one another, compounding a complex problem. Many advanced trauma sufferers are dealing with the destruction of their lives caused by prior trauma-related behaviors. They become less and less equipped to handle the fallout of their behaviors, which only exacerbates their feelings of deep despair and lack of control. A vicious cycle has begun. In combination, these symptoms can be completely overwhelming. Most people at this symptomatic stage reach a breaking point; they are desperate for some relief from their emotional and physical pain.

Trauma symptoms can and do worsen. The potential progression of these symptoms suggests we not delay in getting help for ourselves or for someone we love. Although it can feel otherwise, accepting help is not a moral failing. We are fallible creatures, each and every one of us. For some of us, seeking and asking for help may be the most courageous action we ever take.

CHAPTER 2

Emotional Blueprints and Developmental Trauma

Like many children, I had parents who did not have the tools to be nurturing caretakers. The rejection I felt as a child followed me well into my adult life.

My parents were angry and frightened individuals, and by the time I was a teenager, so was I. Every child longs to feel loved, accepted, and cherished by his or her parents. For many, including myself, that security never comes. We were also extremely poor, and poverty presented a constant threat to the family's survival. The stress of this burden made life in my parents' world a very scary situation.

Growing up in New Jersey in the 1950s as an Orthodox Jew was a dangerous and frightening experience in the first place. Not only did I feel rejected at home by my parents, but my community refused to embrace me as well. I was often abused, verbally and physically, by the neighborhood children—as well as their parents—who detested me because I was Jewish.

Home was an emotionally dangerous place, and the neighborhood wasn't safe either. Yet I preferred the hostility of my neighborhood to the pain and rejection I felt at home with my parents.

Eventually, the streets became my home. I became a violent, angry person whom people feared. Inside, I was as scared as I had ever been. I was terrified of being found out, that someone would learn I was still the vulnerable, frightened child of my youth. A hard exterior was my only choice if I wanted to survive. It would be years before I would find the tools to begin to heal from the effects of the trauma I endured as a child, and the many traumas to follow.

It is an unfortunate reality that parents are often the culprits in the story of developmental trauma. When a child has a parent with habits, tendencies, or urges that create a potentially traumatic environment, the daily events of that child's life can leave him wounded over time. (Parents can also provide the foundation for emotional and psychological growth by demonstrating healthy, balanced behaviors and productive social interactions, but often, this is not the case.) Children desperately need to feel safe and cherished when at home with their parents. When a parent is rejecting, abusive, or creates a hostile, unpredictable environment, such a foundation does not exist for the child. Instead, the foundation of his or her development is characterized by discomfort, fear, and pain. The psychological and physical wounds that come from living in a world where nothing is as it should be are devastating, threatening the very survival of the child.

Parents are not always the culprits. Neighbors, friends, or relatives can also cause harm, intentionally or accidentally. Developmental trauma can begin anywhere, anytime, with anyone.

Children can recover from shock trauma as readily as adults can with appropriate, timely treatment. These same traumatic reactions to isolated events left untreated, however, can cause deeply rooted developmental wounds over time.

Developmental Trauma

When you experience a traumatic event during the developmental stages of your life, the foundation of your psychological growth becomes distorted. By the time you are grown, you may be emotionally handicapped, unable to create or sustain relationships, or unable to manage, much less thrive, in your daily life. Again, *trauma* refers to the damage caused by the event; it does not necessarily describe the nature of the event itself. Seemingly trivial events can have an enormous impact later, affecting every aspect of your life. *Shock* trauma—usually a sudden, one-time event—is most easily identified as "traumatic" by victims as well as by those around them. In these situations, everyone is more likely to recognize the need for treatment and may be more accepting of that need. Traumatic experiences characterized as *developmental* trauma, however, may seem benign and ordinary in comparison, making developmental trauma more difficult to ascertain, and sometimes more difficult to heal from. The symptoms of this trauma can remain dormant in the subconscious mind, emerging later in life to create baffling destruction that seems unrelated to any specific traumatic event.

In such situations, you may not even remember what happened to you; you may not be able to describe what you feel as a result of that experience. You may simply feel that you cannot control the quality of your life and that chaos always is only a heartbeat away. This suggests you may have experienced *developmental trauma*.

A child of divorced parents, for example, may not see the effects of his trauma until well into adulthood. Although divorce is extremely common, children from so-called broken homes are often traumatized by the event. The dramatic change to the life they have always known—with Mom and Dad under the same roof—introduces uncertainty into their lives. The lack of

13

opportunity to observe a functional marriage and learn from those observations can prevent them from interacting productively in their relationships. They may associate marriage with instability and volatility. Such fears can create any number of destructive behaviors that can devastate their relationships and impede their attempts to live a well-adjusted life.

Shock trauma is sometimes associated with developmental trauma. A single, catastrophic event—death of a loved one, an accident, or an assault, for instance—can be devastating for a child, just as it can be for an adult. Children may convincingly conceal the effects of severe trauma, giving us the impression that they are more resilient when, in fact, children are often more susceptible to emotional wounding than adults. Certain events that would have little impact on an adult might be deeply traumatizing for a child.

For example, a patient recounted this story: Alex's estranged father once brought a gun to his mother's home and threatened to hurt them. No one was hurt, but at that moment, Alex felt that his life was in danger. Being a little boy, he became petrified with fear.

As a grown man, Alex exhibits symptoms of trauma, such as substance abuse and disconnectedness. He never received treatment after this terrifying event. If this had been an isolated experience, Alex might have recovered from it. This incident, however, was only one of many damaging elements in his childhood. As well as being a dangerous man, Alex's father was absent for most of Alex's life. Rationally, the absence of a dangerous father may be a blessing, but for a child, that absence often creates additional psychological wounding.

From a therapeutic point of view, developmental trauma is differentiated from shock trauma for a very important reason. Classical developmental trauma occurs over time. Children might experience smaller traumas on a regular basis, even daily, in the forms of neglect, abuse, or other potentially damaging events. Such elements in the child's environment can actually cause *physiological distortions* in her development because she is still in the early phase of her emotional, physical, and cerebral growth. Psychological development—or the lack of it—is considered by some to be irreversible. Early traumas can be challenging to treat and heal; nevertheless, our experience shows that healing is possible with the right treatment.

Lingering Effects

Developmental trauma can produce an avalanche of highly destructive symptoms and behaviors, from emotional withdrawal, depression, and anxiety to intense anger, aggressiveness, and rage. As noted earlier, it can also lead to eating disorders, substance abuse, addiction, insomnia, sexual dysfunction, and attention deficit hyperactivity disorder (ADHD). There is no limit to the potential negative impact created by developmental trauma if it goes untreated and unresolved.

A traumatic event or series of events in childhood changes the direction of a child's development and distorts his or her identity. The event is often folded under layer upon layer of experiences, learned behaviors and habits, and memories that have been altered by a traumatic history. Those afflicted may have to dig through years of development to find the smoking gun—the individual's key to becoming well.

It takes time, patience, and diligence, but developmental trauma can be healed with the correct approach, accurate information, and, in most cases, a skilled psychotherapist. A healthy foundation can be reconstructed. If you are a victim of developmental trauma, you might feel discouraged in the process, but know that healing *is* attainable.

Failed Coping Methods—Addiction and Reenactment

Addiction is a very common symptom among trauma victims of all kinds. It is so widespread that I would say the vast majority of people with substance abuse problems have a traumatic past. There are several schools of thought regarding the causes of addiction. Some call it a disease. Others say it is genetic. These theories may indeed be factors in substance abuse. Trauma, however, seems to be a common denominator among addicts.

Trauma burdens its victims with physical and emotional pain. It also leaves us with an unresolved, trapped "energy," which is residue from an incomplete stress response. This physiological response is discussed in detail in chapter 3.

The discomfort caused by symptoms such as anxiety and pain can be excruciating, and many trauma sufferers desperately need an escape. Drugs, alcohol, or prescription drugs are often the only sources of relief for them because these substances literally numb the pain. They dull the emotions. They provide an escape from negative thoughts and worries. Trauma victims can once again feel "normal" and forget about the painful events in their lives when they use these coping tools.

Trauma victims who become addicts are often physiologically and psychologically dependent on the substance. At first, the use of such a coping strategy may be fueled by an emotional cycle. Addicts use chemical substances to subdue the pain. When the effects of the drug wear off, the pain returns, and they feel compelled to use again. Over time, they may build up physiological addictions as well, ever-raising their tolerance of the substance. Use then multiplies as they look for it to give them the relief it once provided. When a chemical dependency develops, the body begins to scream louder for the drug once the high subsides.

Emotional pain and trauma are the primary reasons so many addicts fail to overcome their substance abuse problems. Even if they find help for their physiological dependencies, their psychological and emotional dependencies soon rise to the surface. The most successful rehabilitation and detoxification programs provide trauma treatment as well as addiction therapy. Unfortunately, many do not offer this, and the underlying trauma—unaddressed—continues to obstruct a full recovery.

The abuse of prescription drugs may not have the same stigma as illegal drug abuse or alcoholism, but it is just as common, if not more so, and it is just as destructive. Many people depend on prescription medications for relief in the same way that others might turn to a bottle of vodka. Prescription drug use is less often questioned; its use may be easier to conceal, and it is legal. Prescription drugs also give many trauma victims the ability to function; they numb the pain and relieve the victim of painful memories. These drugs may temporarily alleviate the pain, but they do not *cure* trauma. There are circumstances in which chemical therapy is necessary and appropriate, but drugs are not a long-term solution for trauma sufferers.

Reenactment occurs when traumatized individuals try to recreate or relive their traumatic experience. They seek out or even create scenarios similar to their traumatizing event in an unconscious attempt to *complete* the stress response that was interrupted so that they can resolve their post-traumatic disorder. Similar experiences re-engage the stress response, the unfinished biological process that left them traumatized in the first place. Victims seek opportunities to engage the stress response in order to complete it, most often unaware of why they are doing so. The trapped energy causes so much emotional and physical pain that the unconscious aspect of trauma victims' brains will go to any lengths to release that energy. Unaware of the process, they may even feel puzzled as to why the same painful events happen to them over and over again.

Victims of rape, incest, or molestation, for example, always experience severe trauma symptoms. You might expect sexual abuse victims to avoid sexual contact because it is too painful, and many of them do. But some victims of rape and sexual abuse exhibit reenactment behaviors. Instead of withdrawing from sexual experiences, they become promiscuous and reckless with their sexuality.

For instance, a patient named Caroline had never exhibited promiscuous behavior until she was date-raped. After a night out with a group of friends, she woke up the next morning in a strange place. She had been drugged and sexually assaulted. Within a few months of this tragic event, Caroline's sexual behavior changed dramatically. She actively pursued sexual encounters, one-night stands, and unsafe sex. She took a 180-degree turn from who she was before the incident.

Caroline's traumatic experience didn't necessarily change her attitudes about sex. In fact, she feels extreme shame following each sexual encounter. But, that doesn't stop her from pursuing them. She feels a magnetic pull toward sexual experiences because she unconsciously needs to complete the final stages of the stress response.

Other victims of sexual assault cope by avoiding sex, relationships, and intimacy at all costs. Interactions that are even remotely similar to their traumatic event are terrifying and unbearable. They live in fear of sexual encounters and may take measures to deter sexual advances, such as avoiding romantic relationships or even altering their appearance to be less attractive.

Changes in sexual behavior as a symptom of trauma can work as an addiction or as reenactment. Sexual addictions may not have anything to do with an extreme sexual appetite. Rather, that appetite may develop as a means to escape the pain they feel elsewhere. While engaged in the sex act, many people forget their problems, past and present. It can feel like a high, much like using drugs or alcohol. But as soon as it's over, those troubles return.

Reenactment is certainly not limited to sexual traumas. Children who were abandoned by a parent or who went through the divorce of their parents may also reenact this experience in future relationships. They will often set themselves up to be abandoned or abused by seeking out friendships and romantic attachments in which they are destined to be left, discarded, or rejected.

Men will become attached to women who are certain to leave them, or they will adopt behaviors that drive women away. Women will form attractions to men who are unattainable, abusive, or noncommittal. They approach life with the mentality that they are always doomed to be abandoned and create real-life situations in which that belief is validated.

Another patient, Lucy, for example, grew up in a home in which her father left her mother for another woman when she was a little girl. Her parents divorced, and Lucy was raised by her mother who did her best as a single parent. When Lucy was old enough to date, she developed a pattern of pursuing boys who weren't really interested in dating her. She would manage to persuade them to date her for a while until they finally, inevitably, broke up with her. She would be devastated every time.

As an adult pursuing more serious relationships, Lucy continues to be involved with men who don't value her, who cheat on her, and who eventually leave her. She doesn't understand why her dating life is this way. Lucy attributes it to the immorality of men and to her worth as a woman. The truth is that there are plenty of men in the world who could love and cherish Lucy, but she is blind to these individuals because of her experience with her father. He was supposed to love and cherish her, but instead, he left her behind. Lucy doesn't know how to build a healthy relationship with a man. She only knows how to experience the pain of her father's leaving over and over again.

It is important to remember that reenactment does not occur on a conscious level. Rather, these patterns surface as a result of the pain and turmoil felt on a subconscious level. And because we do not actively choose these patterns, we are unable to actively choose something different. For the most part, reenactments rarely succeed in completing the energy discharge so desired; instead, they cause additional despair and pain in our lives. Usually after much pain, we discover they are false solutions.

Why does trauma take such a firm hold on our emotional, psychological, and physical well-being? Emotional and psychological experiences have biological and physiological counterparts. In the next chapter, we will take a closer look at how the effects of trauma invade our bodies and remain there.

CHAPTER 3

Trauma and Your Body

In our psychologically aware world, trauma is a popular term. The common man understands that traumatic life events—such as combat, illness, or near-death experiences—can be psychologically damaging. He may even be able to trace the difficulties in his life to a specific event in his past. Something happened, and from that moment on, life was different. He was different.

Most people understand trauma as a simple cause and effect: An event takes place, and psychological and emotional responses follow. But few people understand precisely *why* these events have such an impact in our lives. As a result, victims of trauma often feel confused and powerless about their situation.

Emotional trauma is exactly that: emotional. Humans can have emotional and psychological reactions to devastating life events. But these psychological reactions are actually caused by physiological responses to the experience. When we experience traumatic life events, our bodies go through an involuntary response designed to help us survive that event. When the physiological response does not come to a necessary and natural conclusion, the psychological, emotional, and physical reactions that follow are known as trauma.

The Stress Response

The stress response, also known as the "fight, flight, or freeze" response, is an instinctual reaction to a perceived threat. All living things are programmed to engage the stress response that enables us to fight, flee, or even "play dead" in an effort to survive. Lizards, dogs, and humans—we all have the stress response in common. The experiences that initiate it might be different, but reptiles, mammals, and humans respond to danger in the same way.

In the animal world, the stress response enables prey to escape the predator. You have seen the stress response in action many times. For example, a white-tailed deer is grazing in a field when it hears something in the brush. It senses danger and goes into a hyper-alert state, known as hyper-arousal. This is the beginning of the stress response, in which senses are heightened, heart rate increases, and the deer prepares to flee an attacker. The deer is right, and a cougar charges out of the brush. The deer flees, running at top speed. The reaction is instant.

In a situation like this, there are two possible outcomes: Either the deer gets away or he doesn't. If the deer escapes, the cougar might not get to eat, and the deer lives to engage the stress response another day. When the chase is over and he is out of danger, the deer must come down, or "thaw out," from the hyper-arousal state. This is the final stage of the stress response.

If the deer is caught, he goes into a dissociative state, in which he disconnects psychologically from his body. The dissociative state has two functions. The first is a final effort to escape death in the event that the predator loses interest. The second function is to prevent the prey from feeling pain as it is ripped to shreds. The state is death-like, and the deer feels nothing even as it is eaten alive by the cougar. But if the cougar gives up on the dead-looking deer, the deer will eventually reemerge from the dissociative state and continue with releasing the trapped energy, completing the natural stress response process.

Humans go through the same stages of the stress response during a traumatic experience. Whether it's a car crash, a military experience, or the loss of a loved one, the stress response engages as if we were a deer darting through a forest. In a traumatic moment, we tap into our most primitive, animalistic selves. But humans are not as adept at shaking off the repercussions of the experience; the restrictions it causes can remain in the body, wreaking havoc for many years to follow.

A Biological Process

How does the body know when and how to engage the stress response? As humans, we filter the world around us through a process of rational thoughts and feelings. We see or hear something, and we have emotional and psychological responses. Like animals, we also experience the world through our senses— sight, touch, sound—and our ability to do this depends upon our nervous system.

Reactions such as the stress response are controlled by the autonomic nervous system. The autonomic nervous system is made up of two opposing systems—the sympathetic nervous system and the parasympathetic nervous system. The parasympathetic nervous system engages when the environment is safe and relaxed. We are not on alert and can respond calmly to things happening around us. However, the sympathetic nervous system serves an entirely different function: to launch the stress response and enable us to react quickly to stimuli. The two systems are designed to work in harmony, with the sympathetic nervous system spurring us to action when necessary and the parasympathetic nervous system putting on the brakes.

During the stress response, the sympathetic nervous system has full control of one's body. It switches on when the first shock of danger is detected, or the first moment the deer sensed the cougar in the grass. This initiates the hyper-alert state, characterized by brain signals to the body, causing muscle contractions, acute alertness, and attention to the environment.

As the intensity of the situation increases, the sympathetic nerves begin discharging massive amounts of energy into the body to support the fighting or fleeing about to take place. The nervous system triggers the release of adrenaline and other neurochemicals and hormones. These substances are extremely powerful and enable animals and humans alike to do incredible things. A mother can lift a car to free her child trapped underneath. A man might successfully jump out of a window to escape fire. Because of overwhelming amounts of energy, we can do things during the stress response that we wouldn't normally be able to do.

Even during the dissociative state, energy and adrenaline course through the body. The deer appears dead, but its heart is racing, its blood is pumping, and its body is working on overdrive. Yet, it is perfectly still. The intensity of trauma can be compared to hitting the brakes and flooring the gas in your car at the same time. The car is perfectly still, but there's a tornado under the hood.

The energy overload during the stress response affects the body significantly. Many bodily functions and systems are heightened during the stress response. The heart and lungs work overtime. Blood vessels constrict. Digestion and sexual function can be significantly slowed or even stopped. If prolonged, the stress response can suppress the immune system. Overall, normal functioning is put on hold during the stress response so the body can focus on the task at hand: surviving or coping with the moment.

Needless to say, the stress response is very intense and puts a lot of strain on the body. It can't go on forever. In addition, once the threat is gone, all of that surplus energy has to go somewhere. At this stage, the body must discharge and decompress this excess energy; then, the parasympathetic nervous system can reengage, returning the body and mind to a calm, serene state. Animals and humans are designed to discharge the extra energy, a state sometimes referred to as "thawing out." Trembling, shaking, and twitching serve to release the energy and are visible characteristics of the thawing out stage.

The trembling phase is perhaps the most important step in recovering from a traumatic experience. The supercharged energy is released, the heart rate decreases, and the animal–or human— returns to a normal, relaxed state of consciousness. He is aware of his surroundings but not hyperaware. Once the trembling stops, the energy is fully discharged and the parasympathetic nervous system has resumed its control over the body and the mind.

Animals such as the deer described above almost always complete the thawing out process and return to normal, healthy functioning. They don't have nightmares about being chased by a cougar. They resume life as if the traumatic event never happened, until the next time. And when that day comes, they will be just as capable—both psychologically and physically—of escaping their attacker.

If animals can engage the stress response many times throughout their life without psychological wounding, and humans and animals have so much in common, why are so many people emotionally and physically crippled by traumatic experiences? The difference is the rational human brain, the thing that separates the human world from the animal world. We humans can interrupt and override the stress response, leaving behind intense energy that wreaks havoc on the body and the mind. In fact, a significant percentage of people who have experienced traumatic events suffer lasting psychological and physical damage.

Our Animal Brains

Your heart doesn't beat only sometimes. Your stomach doesn't decide whether to finish digesting your food. And we don't rationalize whether to fight or flee in a stressful situation. It just happens. The more primitive parts of our brain demand it. Not all parts of the human brain function at the same level of complexity and sophistication. The human brain includes elements of primitive functionality that enable us to operate on an instinctive, survival level.

Every animal, including humans, has what is known as the "reptilian brain." The reptilian brain allows animals and humans to act instinctively and automatically. For example, a reptile functions from instinct alone, and every move it makes comes from the need to survive. The reptile eats, flees, and adapts automatically, without hesitation or rationalization. Survival is its only objective.

The reptilian brain generates immediate responses. It contains an entire framework and code for survival. The reptile's days are spent finding food, finding shelter, and avoiding danger because the reptile is commanded solely by the reptilian brain. It has little need for social interaction or emotion. The creature that functions on instinct lives a simple life. However, instinct and the reptilian brain are also components of more complex and sophisticated creatures.

Animals and humans have a more complex brain structure—in addition to the reptilian brain—known as the limbic system. The limbic system enables us to build on the instinctive commands of the reptilian brain in a way that gives us our social and emotional natures. The limbic system allows animals to bond together in

26

groups and maintain social systems to improve survival or create learned behaviors and strategies from past experiences. The limbic part of the brain itself is influenced by instinctual urges, but it also enables animals to develop sophisticated behaviors to address those urges. More importantly, it is the precursor to the rational part of the brain that separates humans from animals.

Humans rely a great deal on our rational brain structure, also known as the neo-cortex. The neo-cortex is the most sophisticated brain structure in existence and enables conscious thought, the decision-making process, language, and rationalization. The rational ability of the human neo-cortex is so highly developed that it can even override some of the most primal instincts, including the stress response.

It's hard to believe that we can rationalize our way out of basic instinct. But the neo-cortex is very powerful. Humans frequently interrupt their own stress response processes—or someone else might interrupt it. As a result, the surplus energy is never discharged and continues to circulate in the body. Over time, that energy wears down the body. The body thinks it's still in the midst of the traumatic event and so does the mind, even on a subconscious level.

A stress response override can happen to anyone, even seasoned psychotherapists. I recently saw a horrific car accident while driving with my wife. I pulled over to help and immediately went into hyper-arousal in order to do what needed to be done to save the people as quickly as possible. It was a life-or-death situation. The victims were severely wounded. One victim had been thrown from the car, and I had to pull him off the road. Needless to say, it was an overwhelming experience.

Paramedics arrived and I went on my way, knowing the victims were in good hands. Intellectually, I knew I should give myself time to come down from my experience, to thaw out. But I told myself it was no big deal, that I was fine, and that I needed to get back on the road. Even as I drove, my heart pounded, and the surplus of intense energy eventually made me physically ill. Only when I had to pull over because I thought I might vomit did I realize what I had done. I then took as much time as I needed to relax and return to a calm, normal state. If I hadn't, I could very well have been traumatized by this experience.

That is exactly what happens when people become traumatized. The stress response is a highly intense reaction that requires massive amounts of energy. It is the most intense psychological and physiological experience humans can have. While the powerful energy of the stress response is intended to save lives, the energy becomes toxic if it is not discharged. We can use a household appliance as a metaphor for this process. Your refrigerator, computer, hairdryer, or television is nothing more than a heap of plastic or steel without the energy it requires to function. If too much energy is provided, however, a surge of electricity can permanently damage any of these things. Although there is more to the human makeup than to that of household gadgets, human beings function much the same way. The human body consists of tissue, bone, cells, and water. But electrical impulses play a significant role in putting all of this matter into motion. The brain uses a type of electricity, much like a computer does, to tell your body what to do, from giving a hug to breathing. This use of the appropriate amount of electricity is essential to human function on every level. The stress response, however, can be likened to a power surge. With too much energy trapped in the body and nowhere for it to go, things start to break down. Unresolved energetic responses cause further trauma, and the results can be devastating.

Although developmental traumas are sometimes characterized as milder stressors occurring regularly in younger years, the stress response of the sympathetic nervous system is in full force, regardless. Less dramatic events can still engage the hyper-alert state, keeping young people in a constant state of hyper-arousal with the excess energy never fully discharging. As the individuals mature, the surplus energy distorts their development, both physically and psychologically. The events of developmental trauma may be less dramatic than shock trauma, but the effects can be much more damaging.

As long as the trapped energy of an unresolved response remains, the victim will continue to suffer painful emotional and psychological symptoms—and often, physical symptoms as well. The good news is that this trapped energy can be freed, even years later. The key to recovering from the injuries of traumatic experience of all kinds is to address the healing of mind *and* body. In my experience, classical talk therapy is only one aspect of successful treatment; we must address the physical vestiges of traumatic experience as well. We must find a way to "release" this trapped energy or the intrusion of traumatic symptoms will be inevitable. It will become a portion of our cellular memory, hiding in microscopic trenches in our bodies and brains.

For those suffering the effects of trauma, we have found a revolutionary way to free this trapped energy—though it has been a long time in coming—to bring resolution to the interrupted stress response that lurks beneath the surface, making true healing possible for victims of trauma.

CHAPTER 4

Finding a Solution

My street-smart survival tactics took me to New York, where I began climbing my way up the financial ladder. In the meantime, my father had been climbing his own ladder. The financial burdens that characterized my youth were long gone; my father had established a flourishing commercial construction business in New Jersey. Almost overnight, he became a wealthy man, although the emotional problems that burdened our family remained.

The good fortune that my father found on the Jersey Shore would soon take a dangerous turn, however. When my father refused to surrender a portion of his profits to the local network of organized crime, we found ourselves in a threatening public battle. Very few people challenged this organization, but my father and I eventually risked everything—even our lives—to fight a war that we could not win. We were too foolish to see that this feud could only end tragically.

I do not look back on this time in my life with pride. At the time, I thought I was the hero. In reality, I became a man nearly as threatening as the criminals I was fighting, yet I was no match for the intensity of this organization. I was still in denial about my own vulnerability and limited strength; I thought I could take on this enemy alone. This went on for years. I was tough, angry, and terrified underneath it all. I had grown accustomed to the pain.

Miraculously, an accountant with whom I'd done business–merely an acquaintance, though I had known him awhile–decided to have an open, honest conversation with me about the path I was on. He knew these people intimately. He knew what I was too afraid to admit to myself: I could not survive the conflict in which I was embattled for much longer. I was in very dangerous territory. He advanced me my annual tax refund and suggested (none too vaguely) that I go as fast and as far away from New Jersey as possible, never to return.

He also knew that I inspired a great loyalty in those who worked for me and that I genuinely cared about people. He thought I should consider going back to college to study psychology. "You could be a good therapist," he said. This was far beyond anything I had envisioned for myself; it just wasn't part of my reality on the Jersey Shore. But, when I left the East Coast shortly thereafter, I began to seriously consider his far-fetched suggestion. And by the time I arrived on the West Coast, I had decided to take his advice. I soon discovered that he had not only saved my life; he had given me a new one.

An Opportunity to Heal

I had a new identity and a fresh start. California, the new frontier, was an opportunity for drastic change, and I seized it. My basic training at Fort Ord in Monterey during the Viet Nam war era had introduced me to Northern California, and I decided to return to the area. I began to explore my interest in psychology and therapy, looking for a way to put my talents to use and hoping to find a positive way to be productive and helpful to others.

I enrolled in the university to pursue an education, something I previously would not have considered doing, and I fell in love with learning. Eventually, I began working in group homes and juvenile treatment facilities in Santa Clara and San Mateo counties while continuing my education at San Jose and San Francisco state universities. I was introduced to the work of many psychologists and psychotherapists at these institutions, but as my education intensified, one in particular caught my attention. His name was Wilhelm Reich, the founder of something called "somatic psychology."

Reich, a protégé of Sigmund Freud, introduced the idea that the body, as well as the mind, harbored subconscious memories, pain, and experiences. He was the first to bring the body into psychoanalysis and to physically touch his patients. This was considered radical at the time, but Reich contended that emotional healing could not be fully achieved without addressing the body and its physical healing. Although some of his initial approaches to what is now called "bodywork" seemed peculiar, the foundation of his theories was brilliant. In fact, I *knew* it to be valid.

Quite suddenly, it was obvious that the story of my painful past remained in my body. I carried myself as if I were always on the defense. My chest was hard, and even the slightest pressure was excruciating. I now recognized this as an example of what Reich called "armoring." Armoring is the sum total of the muscular attitudes that a person develops as a defense against the breaking-through of emotions, especially anxiety, rage, and sexual excitation. This can be accompanied by what he called "character armor," the sum total of all the years of defensive emotional attitudes that have also been incorporated in the person's character. Physical armoring involves the hardening of fascia—the connective tissue covering or binding together parts of the body—due to unreleased tension. *Characterological armoring,* or an armoring of one's attitude, often accompanies the physiological process. The term *character* is defined by the ways

33

in which a person typically acts and responds to the world around him. These responses can become rigid as a reaction to trauma in the same way that the fascia becomes inflexible.

Wilhelm Reich
Armoring - Seven Segments of the Body

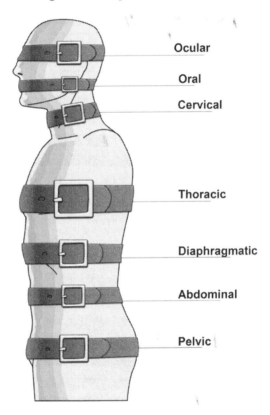

Ocular

Oral

Cervical

Thoracic

Diaphragmatic

Abdominal

Pelvic

This illustration shows the binding effects of armoring. According to Reich, armoring is the major obstacle to growth. Armoring can be thought of as the juncture between body and mind that causes abnormal behavior. It limits a person's ability to feel, think, act, and relate to others. It's like a mental, physical, and emotional straitjacket that compromises an individual's reactions to life and reduces the ability to function in the world.

Characterological armoring can be just as debilitating as physical armoring. Some might argue that characterological armoring is even more destructive than physical armoring because it more readily affects the lives and relationships of those around the armored individual. Instead of reacting rationally and thoughtfully in relationships with others, those suffering from characterological armoring can be harsh and even abusive. They may withdraw emotionally from their lives or relationships or may develop irrational phobias. Their responses and demeanor can become exaggerated and aggressive. The reason people behave this way is not that they have carefully calculated the benefits of their actions; rather, these are knee-jerk reactions rooted in the unconscious, designed to protect them from further pain and damage.

Armoring seldom achieves the desired results, however. We are never completely protected from the heartaches of life no matter how armored we may be. Physical and characterological armoring usually leave a person *more* vulnerable to pain and rejection, and his behavior can become increasingly dysfunctional and ineffective as a consequence. Victims of trauma do not choose this physical state or the behavior it produces. It is chosen for them by the involuntary nature of armoring. Armoring—both physical and characterological—is a natural and inevitable human response to trauma. As with breathing, digesting food, and blinking, we do not decide to armor ourselves. It happens without our permission because we have had experiences that triggered our bodies and brains to defend themselves.

Just as it is involuntary, armoring is inherently defensive. It is often defined as an adaptive, preemptive strike against the most painful elements of our lives. We develop behaviors, actions, and reactions that form an emotional and psychological barrier around us to keep away those who could do us harm—on any level. We feel desperate to protect ourselves from the pain we carry inside as well. Unlike most instinctual acts of defense and protection, armoring leaves us *less* prepared to deal with future hardships.

It is highly unlikely that armoring will disappear without treatment. It is a chronic condition that rarely heals itself. Many people are destined to cope with the ramifications of their secret defense systems for their entire lives. We can free ourselves of armoring, however, by enlisting the help of a trained therapist and bodyworker who has a thorough understanding of the mind-body connection. Only then can we begin to release the toxic tension that is bringing the pain of the past into the present.

Reich's methodology employed bodywork that he hoped would address the attributes referred to as armoring, which is so often associated with trauma. His approach has since served as a basis for gentler, more effective methods of healing trauma that are, in my experience, exponentially more successful than either Reich's initial methods or classic talk therapy alone. I have also discovered, as Reich did, that our bodies are more sophisticated than we can imagine, and they are in tune with our minds at a deeply emotional level.

Physician—Heal Thyself

I continued my studies, enrolling in a Ph.D. program and working in a hospital psych-ward for three years; I was eventually directing a drug and alcohol treatment center. I was well on my way to creating a new life for myself. At the same time, however, it seemed the life I thought I had left in New Jersey was lurking around every corner. I couldn't get comfortable in my own skin. I walked around with an armored exterior, always ready for battle even when there was nothing and no one to fight. My marriage of eight years soon failed. There may have been other issues, but in retrospect, I see that I could not turn off my anger and defensiveness. I was no longer choosing that behavior; it was choosing me. The fear and anger of my former life were in charge of me despite the fact that there was no need for them in my new environment.

As I learned more about my own psychological makeup and the power of psychotherapy, it became clear to me that although I had great interest in helping others deal with their lives, it was time to find some help for myself. How could I encourage others to confront their pain and deal with their experiences when my own unresolved issues were controlling me? For the first time in my life, I was able to acknowledge my difficulties, and I made the decision to seek the help needed to resolve them.

For many of us, acknowledging that we are burdened by our pasts can be the most difficult part of getting help. I finally took that challenging step. My recovery was no doubt delayed because I had trouble finding a therapist whom I could respect. Extremely distrustful, I had an unreasonable fear of appearing or feeling weak. I didn't want to be made to feel that I didn't have the skills or the strength to survive in the world. My physical and mental strength had been my security blanket for most of my life. Therapists who lacked physical and emotional presence were, in my eyes, ill equipped to take me on. I knew that if a therapist doesn't appear to be a credible and respectable source, the process has little value for the patient. (See chapter 6, "Seeking Treatment," for more information about this.) I went through numerous professionals, all of whom were powerless to give me the help I needed. Usually, I made up my mind about them within seconds of meeting them. Then, I met Dr. Gerald Frank, and that all changed.

Dr. Frank was an imposing figure in every way, from his physical presence to his demeanor. He did not fit the traditional mold of a therapist—at least, none I had met. He embraced a therapeutic approach that was uncommon in the early '70s, a form of Reichian psychotherapy that definitely took a backseat to the humanistic psychology and personal growth movement popular at that time. Most therapists were probing the minds of their patients with methods emerging from this movement, but Gerry, as I came to call him, employed the ideas of Wilhelm Reich. Immediately I could tell that he was able to see my pain and experiences clearly. My wounds were decades old, but this man knew how to unearth them and bring them into the light. I had at last met my match.

As I began to explore these ideas with Gerry as my therapist, mentor, and later, dear friend, my body began to relax and unwind; it felt as if something had been unlocked, and the emotional prison I was in began to fall away.

I spent the next two decades learning about and practicing this revolutionary approach to therapy and the body. I began to see remarkable changes in my patients. In addition, it took them considerably less time to recover from trauma using these methods than with traditional therapy.

As I grew confident in the foundation of this approach to healing trauma, I wondered whether there was a way to expand on these ideas, a way to make these innovative healing tools even more effective. The desire to provide my patients with even greater healing would soon lead me into the world of physical therapy and would revolutionize my practice.

CHAPTER 5

Taking It to the Next Level

As I began to work with more and more victims of traumatic experience over the years, I hoped to find a key to the vast human capacity for resilience that I sensed was still untapped by professional therapists. As valuable as I found the therapy introduced to me by Gerry Frank, it fell short of the *optimal* physical and emotional healing that I knew in my heart was possible. We had scratched the surface—indeed, we had gone deeper than most of our peers—but I sensed there was more we could do to alleviate the pain suffered by victims of trauma. And given what we had learned from our literally "hands on" experience, I suspected the key to further healing lay in the body itself.

If you have ever had a professional massage or visited the chiropractor, you may have noticed more than physical improvements after your visit. Immediately following certain kinds of bodywork, patients sometimes find that forgotten memories resurface. You may experience memories and emotions— both positive and negative—that have long since been repressed. You may be aware that mental and emotional shifts have taken place during your session, even though verbal interaction with the professional was limited.

Such results may surprise you if you enlisted the help of a massage therapist (or other physical therapist) to address only physical pain or misalignment. If you wanted to work on your emotional health, you would have called a psychotherapist, right? These unexpected emotional experiences can open a Pandora's

Box of emotion that is either unsettling or simply interesting, sparking a curiosity about what is hidden in your unconscious mind.

Various forms of physical therapy are designed to address the body and nothing more. They are intended to resolve physical ailments and restore the body to normal flexibility and range of motion as well as a healthy alignment of the spine. But as we have noted, manipulating the body can lead to an unintentional excavation of the mind. While many therapists of various practices are trained to expect emotional reactions to their work, many are not trained to provide psychotherapy. Because their professional training ends with physiology, patients may be left with unanswered questions, concerns, and, sometimes, feelings of raw emotional experience and memory.

Massage therapists, chiropractors, and other bodywork specialists offer a valuable service and play an important role in the process of physical—and emotional—healing; however, patients who pursue bodywork without a psychotherapeutic counterpart will likely experience short- or long-term relief for their physical pain and nothing more. Issues for the patient and the practitioner arise when emotions come to the surface and the practitioner is without tools to address them. Patients are extremely vulnerable in this situation, which could result in further exposure to trauma if they do not seek additional help from an appropriate source.

After a number of years applying what I had learned about healing the effects of trauma, I began to look for ways to refine and strengthen the approach that I had been using, a version of the therapy introduced to me by Gerry. Wilhelm Reich had known that the body and mind were connected in a way that he could not fully understand, and I knew that the many links between mind and body were yet to be discovered. However, I knew that I had a valuable start in the right direction, and I continued to follow my intense interest in how emotions and experiences affect the physical body. This led me to John Barnes, a gifted physical therapist and trainer.

John Barnes had significantly refined a physical therapy style that he called myofascial release therapy (MFR), which was originally developed by Andrew Taylor Still and others. I had read that patients undergoing MFR were experiencing some of the physical and emotional relief that I saw in my current practice without any associated psychoanalytical or verbal therapy. Patients were reporting an impressive level of emotional healing from this physical therapy alone. As a self-identified Reichian psychotherapist, I was already convinced that the body and the mind were connected in a very complex way, so I wasted no time arranging to meet John Barnes in person so that I could find out what myofascial release therapy was all about. I attended one of his workshops in Sedona, Arizona.

When I arrived, I met a woman named Christy who was also there to learn about using MFR in the treatment of trauma victims; as an exercise, I was to practice the techniques I was learning in this workshop while she acted as my patient. Christy was a memorable example of someone suffering the consequences of armoring, and she knew it. Some people live with extremely debilitating cases of armoring for many years.

As I began the movements and techniques I was learning, a mass that looked like a tumor emerged from Christy's abdominal area. We were both alarmed, but at the instructor's request, I continued with the gentle movements. The mass began to move, as did Christy, who shortly thereafter started thrashing, twisting, and writhing so fiercely that I thought surely I was doing more harm than good. Again, I was encouraged to continue, and after a short time, Christy stood up; her body posture and alignment had dramatically changed for the better. The mass was gone.

In talking with her afterward, I learned that a car in a grocery store parking lot had hit Christy a few years earlier. Even though her doctors had assured her that she was supposedly healed, she had been in near-constant pain since the accident, and her quality of life had deteriorated enormously. She explained to me that during our session, she had relived every instant of that accident.

Doctors had carefully treated Christy's physical injuries, but the emotional trauma she experienced was not addressed. She couldn't understand why her life suddenly seemed to veer out of control, her relationships suffered, and she felt physically ill. The traumatic nature of her accident produced a reaction that was physical as well as emotional. A mass of tissue—a knotted lump of *fascia* that had been buried in her gut—was now gone. This constriction had affected the alignment of her body and her overall physical, emotional, and even spiritual health, retaining the memory of the accident and the unresolved energetic response to her trauma.

One-time events such as Christy's experience of being hit by a car, however, are not the only kind of situations that can produce armoring. Experiences that occur over time during our formative years (developmental trauma) can produce armoring as well.

I once treated a patient named Lisa who had experienced tremendous rejection and abandonment by her mother as a little girl. When Lisa was young, her mother decided that she didn't want to be a part of their family anymore and left. Her mother did take Lisa's two younger sisters along with her, however, and left Lisa behind. Naturally, Lisa felt unwanted and less valuable than her two siblings. Throughout her life, Lisa made countless attempts to win her mother's approval only to experience rejection over and over again.

When I first met Lisa, even before I learned about her painful relationship with her mother, her physical armoring was obvious to me. She was overweight. She dealt with chronic, excruciating headaches as well as tightness and constriction in her chest. She also demonstrated a cynical attitude and consistently pursued men who rejected her. When the time came to apply the physical part of our therapy, even the slightest pressure on Lisa's chest was agonizing. She literally could not bear the weight of a feather on her chest.

It may sound highly symbolic, but Lisa had literally developed armoring in her chest to protect her from the pain of a broken heart. The reality is that her heart had been "broken" many times over by her mother's rejection. The negative energy from her traumatic childhood and relationship with her mother became locked in her chest, where the fascia became stiff and hardened. She instinctively defended herself physically and emotionally from her own pain through the armoring around her heart.

Christy's and Lisa's experiences are very different, and so are their armoring patterns. But regardless of the differences, both women developed armoring as a result of their traumatic experiences. They did not make a conscious decision to armor themselves—it was their body's innate defense response. In Lisa's case, armoring was a way of coping with and adapting to the chronic, painful experiences in her life. In Christy's case, the surge of energy from her near-death experience was never discharged and became locked in her fascial system to create a tumor-like mass of fascial tissue. Lisa and Christy experienced trauma in very different ways, but the result was the same.

My introduction to myofascial release therapy helped me take Reichian therapy to a level I had long envisioned. MFR therapy introduced a working knowledge of the fascial system, and, for me, revealed the key behind the mysterious mind-body connection. Reich's approach to physical therapy was often too aggressive for patients suffering from significant trauma and emotional pain. MFR provided a gentler, more sensitive approach to physical therapy that was much more effective. I decided to combine the best of what I had learned from Reichian therapy and the techniques of myofascial release therapy in my practice.

To say it was a turning point in my practice would be an understatement. It radically redirected my approach to helping victims of trauma (including me) heal to a degree previously impossible. Using this combination of therapies, which we now refer to as Reichian myofascial release therapy (RMFR), we are able to treat patients with even the most extreme cases of physical and psychological abuse, including many combat vets suffering from acute posttraumatic stress disorder. The results have been nothing short of amazing.

Fascia—The Healing Link

The fascia is a vast, web-like system of connective tissue that covers all muscles, organs, nerves, blood vessels, and veins, even penetrating to the cellular level. It acts as a protector and a container.

Healthy fascia should be flexible, pliable, and even stretchy. It should allow your body to move freely without restraint. Otherwise, organs may not function properly due to constriction, and cells may be starved of oxygen. In addition, fascia contains a flow of energy, electrical impulses that allow it to work in sync with your body.

This stretchy, collagenous connective tissue is also incredibly tough. Its strength and density would suggest that the human body could retain its shape and structure even without the skeleton. Some research suggests that fascia has a tensile strength of as much as 2000 pounds per square inch. When we clearly understand how strong this often overlooked structure really is, it is easier to recognize the importance of maintaining its pliability in order to achieve overall health.

Fascia is a network of connective tissues that are both continuous and contiguous throughout the entire body. It has an appearance similar to a spider's web or a sweater. Fascia covers and interpenetrates every muscle, bone, nerve, artery and vein as well as all of our internal organs including the heart, lungs, brain and spinal cord. It is one structure that exists from head to foot without interruption going all the way to the cellular level.

When one part of the body is injured or compromised in any way, it can affect tissues that are far from the original site of the injury or impairment. In the case of repetitive strain injuries, this means that tissue changes in the shoulder which are the result of an old injury can, over time, affect the condition and function of fascia farther down the arm and into the hand. Symptoms may be felt in one area, but the source of the strain could be located somewhere else.

We might expect tissue this durable to be more resistant to change, but in reality, the shape, texture, and health of the fascial system are easily influenced even without enduring any physical trauma. In fact, emotional trauma is the fascial system's worst enemy.

When trauma of either sort occurs, this delicate collagenous system becomes as restrictive and oppressive as a fifteenth-century suit of armor. In these cases, instead of protecting us as it once did, the change in our fascia leaves us vulnerable to additional emotional pain and further trauma.

As illustrated in previous chapters, encountering a traumatic experience causes a surge of energy that, in simplistic terms, becomes trapped and frozen in the body. This constriction is reflected in the fascia, where energy once flowed freely and continuously. The delicate ebb and flow of energy is interrupted at certain points within the tissue, and the supple material becomes hard, twisted, or knotted. In my opinion, the fascial system is the most sophisticated armoring system in existence.

The pressure caused by armoring can lead to a number of physical conditions that significantly diminish one's health and quality of life—menstrual pain, chronic bladder infections, fibromyalgia, and many other illnesses can develop as a result of armoring.

Imagine a jellyfish swimming in the ocean. The jellyfish fluidly expands and contracts as it moves through the water. But if one were to wrap a rubber band around a jellyfish, those once-elegant movements would become strained, erratic, and possibly even frantic. If it lived at all, adapting to life within the confines of the rubber band, the jellyfish would become vulnerable and unhealthy. In a similar way, people may adapt to living with a compromised, hardened fascial system; most are unaware that their fascia is changing, becoming armored.

Physical trauma, of course, can damage any part of the internal body, including the fascial system. In a serious car accident, for example, passengers often sustain physical injuries, both internal and external. While physical injuries often heal completely over time, fascia does not. Even after all physical wounds have healed, fascia will remain in an altered state because it retains the memory of the physical injuries and emotional trauma of the accident. The physical trauma Christy experienced when hit by a car had healed, but she still felt uncomfortable and experienced pain on a daily basis. Unlike much of the body, the fascial system needs assistance to heal.

It can be very difficult to restore fascia to their original state in an effort to liberate the patient from her physical pain and relieve her emotional burdens. Nevertheless, MFR proves to be a valuable tool for unlocking fascial binding to deliver release and relief.

Slow and sustained stretching combined with light pressure at key points proves to be the most successful way to "unwind" and soften the fascial tissue. The success of each technique involved is greatly determined by the length of each stretch. A sustained stretch can enable the tissue's elasticity once more, allowing it to lengthen and loosen.

This aspect of the therapy is often a surprise to those who are new to its techniques, as many physical therapy methods used look quite different from slow, sustained stretching. Additionally, patients might expect their therapist to focus these techniques on the exact part of the body in which they feel the pain or discomfort. The continuous nature of the fascial system, however, can often produce pain or other issues distant from the source of the fascial restriction. Again, fascial tissue touches and surrounds everything in our bodies. When fascia becomes distorted and rigid, it can restrict the functions of organs, muscles, even bones and vessels. And because these elements of the body are dependent on each other, working synergistically together, a fascial restriction in one area can cause dysfunction and pain elsewhere in the body. A knowledgeable therapist may work on an area of the body that seems unrelated to the patient's discomfort but that may in fact be the source of the problem.

As we learn more about fascia and its deeply reactive nature, a portion of the mystery behind the mind-body connection begins to unfold. Armoring was a part of Reich's vocabulary, but fascia was not. He knew that the body had the propensity to physically protect itself as a reaction to intensely emotional and traumatic experiences. It was not clear *which* physical element of the body was responsible for that reaction, and it was a mystery what role the mind had in this process. Understanding the fascial system, however, brings everything into focus. The fascial system is the physical representation of how our emotional lives impact our physical bodies, and armoring is the result of that impact. The process of armoring has physiological and psychological elements that demonstrate a clear connection between emotional and physical health. Addressing these elements in tandem is critical to comprehensive healing.

Reichian Myofascial Release Therapy (RMFR) — A Potent Combination

When the ultimate goal was the healing of emotional wounds, MFR was proving to be one of the most effective forms of body therapy we had ever employed. As my colleagues and I began to integrate the techniques of this effective modality into the type of Reichian psychotherapy we had been refining for years, we discovered that the combination of these two approaches went beyond either MFR or Reichian psychotherapy alone; it created remarkably greater long-term results for patients, many of whom had struggled to overcome emotional and psychological issues their entire lives. We came to call this permutation RMFR—Reichian Myofascial Release therapy.

What makes RMFR unique? Although any therapist who uses bodywork does influence fascia in one way or another, RMFR is a method specifically developed to address the unique physical quality and emotional memory of fascia. Because this modality focuses on "unwinding" and restoring the fascia to a healthy, responsive state, it deals directly with the most memory-rich tissues in the body.

Using RMFR has made thorough healing a real possibility for many patients who desperately want relief from their emotional haunts. The gentle pressure and slow techniques of the therapy create a soothing emotional and physical process while unwinding fascial restrictions. When the tension in the tissue is released, the trapped energy is mobilized, creating the physical and emotional space for memories to surface and heal. As these memories reach the conscious level, the patient may re-experience that event. This process of resolution can provide a final resting place for traumatic events that have continued to cause emotional and physical damage.

As noted earlier in this chapter, it is essential that patients have a therapist skilled in handling the thoughts and experiences arising as a result of this type of treatment.

Although RMFR techniques are gentle, some patients may find that the intensity of the pain they have grown accustomed to feeling increases in the hours following their session. They may also experience pain in new areas of the body as well as temporary nausea or light-headedness. These are normal reactions to this type of therapy and usually subside within a day of each session. Once this initial pain subsides, patients often experience a relief that they have not felt in years.

Many patients report that they feel almost immediate physical and emotional relief from their pain after a session. The time required to achieve permanent relief, however, is determined by how long the restriction has been in place. A long-standing pattern of armoring may require additional sessions to achieve results. Traumatic fascial restrictions incurred more recently may respond fully to unwinding techniques in less time and fewer sessions.

The fascial tissue can also recoil back to restriction following a session. This regression is a normal part of the process, and numerous sessions may be required to establish a new state of normalcy for the tissue. RMFR therapists often recommend specific stretches and exercises that help the tissue remain unwound. Sometimes a minimum of two sessions per week for a prescribed length of time may be suggested to effectively prevent regression of the tissues.

Combining the best, most effective techniques of myofascial release with Reichian psychotherapy to create RMFR has resulted in a cutting-edge method of healing emotional and physical trauma, which, in our experience, has made it possible for patients to reach a level of psychological and physical recovery they never imagined they could achieve. This approach demonstrates that when we allow the mind and body to work together, we can heal the effects of trauma.

It is thrilling to discover what I had always hoped to be true: What once seemed to be permanent damage can be reversed. Psychological wounds from trauma can be healed. All we need to do is break away from the pack, be open to finding a solution, and embrace the miraculous, God-given ability of the human body to heal itself from the inside out. We can reclaim our minds and our bodies and can begin to fully participate in life once again.

CHAPTER 6

Seeking Treatment

If you have ever considered seeking treatment, even if you have yet to follow through with it, I acknowledge your courage. Facing reality and accepting that we need help can be a very difficult and even painful process.

In the United States and in many other nations around the world, we embrace a culture of independence and self-reliance. Accepting help has a stigma that many people aren't comfortable with. But disarming this ideology is an important step that we must take if we want to truly embrace our natural capacity for healing and resilience. The truth is that almost everyone needs help, and they need to be empowered to get it.

Because we are often blind to signs that indicate a much larger, trauma-related issue, many people don't know that they need treatment in the first place. It's easier to ignore the parts of our lives that are dysfunctional than to look at them and think, "Something bigger is going on here." We ignore or deny these problems, which more often than not causes additional damage.

Why Is It So Important to Seek Treatment?

The effects of trauma are cumulative—they can progress and intensify over time. In fact, time does *not* heal all wounds. Trauma left untreated can grow from a manageable problem into a significant one. Time merely gives the effects of trauma the opportunity to fester and cause deeper wounding, both physical and emotional. Trauma-related wounds seldom subside on their own. Many victims require treatment before they can recover from their experiences and restore peace and functionality to their lives. Without treatment, they may spend a lifetime trying to figure out where their lives got off track and why physical and emotional pain seem constant. It's an uncomfortable, if not tragic, existence.

Ultimately, treatment can restore your quality of life and productivity. Almost everyone has a dream or a goal in life. Perhaps our dream is to have a family, write a book, help others, or achieve a certain level in your chosen career. Whatever the goal may be, we choose it because we believe that we will be happy and content when that goal is realized. A life of fulfillment is what most people want, regardless of their achievements. No one wants to be miserable, depressed, or angry, experiencing every day as a struggle. Our goals symbolize something much bigger: the quality of life that we hope to enjoy when they're reached.

When trauma enters the picture, however, and wires get crossed in our physical and emotional network, the train to our goals and dreams derails. Not only can we lose the potential to reach those milestones, but we are denied quality of life in general. Relationships fall apart, health declines, and life can feel overwhelming and out of control. Treatment can restore the order that was undone by the chaos of trauma. We can get our lives back on track and find release from the angst and pain that is constantly present even if we don't know how it happened to us. Treatment can make it possible to once again have the fulfilling lives we deserve.

Happiness, joy, fulfillment, peace—all are abstract terms that may be difficult for us to define. We don't always know when they are present in our lives, but we sure do miss them when they're absent. If you have a history of trauma, it is affecting your current life whether you realize it or not. Treatment is the best way to liberate yourself from a past that prevents you from experiencing the great things in life that are possible. It may sound philosophical, but it has become a reality for many of our patients.

Treatment may also improve your physical health because traumatic experiences can lead to puzzling but serious health problems. As discussed in previous chapters, many symptoms of trauma materialize as more serious diseased states—from insomnia to seizures. In an effort to address these physical issues, patients often look to the medical world for a solution and end up on a wild goose chase for the right medication or medical procedure. What they usually don't hear is that their problem is emotional, or *psychosomatic*, a term that has acquired a negative or shameful connotation. Without treating the emotional wounds, problems most often persist.

Traditional medicine has begun to embrace the notion that stress can compound other issues to produce a myriad of physical repercussions. Instead of emphasizing the destructive nature of trauma-related stress, those in the medical field often recommend that their patients reduce their current-day stress levels. In my opinion, this advice is a naive effort to address the core problem: continuous, long-term stress produced by trauma. Meditation and stress-management may be helpful in coping with daily life, but they aren't likely to resolve old traumas. Many of those suffering spend time, money, and emotion pursuing treatments that will never work. If you want to be truly proactive about your health, addressing your emotional health is as important as diet and regular exercise.

Psychological treatment also has other benefits above and beyond improving your health and your quality of life. Patients undergoing treatment sometimes find that having someone they can trust outside of their family, friends, and social circle to discuss the incidents of their lives, their feelings, and fears—without judgment—is liberating. They look forward to appointments with their therapist. Verbalizing their thoughts and emotions about the difficult things in their life provides release and security. In this setting, they can share things with someone without damaging their other relationships; thus, they gain insight into their own actions and behaviors as well as into the actions and behaviors of those around them.

Treatment can help you move past painful and traumatic experiences that have troubled you all your life. It can illuminate the connection between your current struggles—emotional, physical, spiritual, or otherwise—and a distant, even repressed, event that occurred years or decades earlier. Treatment is a way to heal emotional wounds just as you would nurse a physical wound back to health. It gives you the opportunity to move beyond your traumatic experiences instead of allowing them to define you.

If there is so much to be gained from psychological treatment, why is it that so many shy away from it? *Treatment, therapist, shrink,* and *disorder* are scary words in our society. No one wants to appear to be mentally unstable or "crazy"; people fear that seeking treatment is an indication of that. Many also feel shame around traumatic experiences. They feel a cultural obligation to be strong, and they fear that if they are troubled by these experiences, they are weak. Unfortunately, the stigma of mental and emotional wounding keeps millions of people in need out of treatment.

A glaring example of this is the fact that a disturbingly small percentage of soldiers returning from combat seek psychological treatment after their experiences overseas. They fill out a routine questionnaire, claim that everything is fine, and bypass the immediate opportunity to address a psychological injury that will only become more apparent over time. Yet, an overwhelming percentage of military personnel have traumatic experiences during active duty in a conflict.

Why they would decline the opportunity to get the help offered by the military may be perplexing. But it is a predictable response when you consider the culture of the armed forces, which is based on strength, bravery, and discipline. They are trained to go forth no matter what. The culture is also based on pride and respect, and that is exactly what prevents soldiers from getting the help they desperately need. They are afraid of losing the respect of their comrades, derailing their career, and forever being stigmatized as a weak, incapable soldier who crumbles under his own emotions and cannot be trusted or counted on to perform his duty.

The general population is not so different. People are afraid of being judged by employers, friends, and family members. These expectations and codes of conduct operate just underneath the surface of our consciousness. As a result, innumerable people, including soldiers, nurses, paramedics, firefighters, police officers, and civilians, are in denial about their own need for treatment.

Some traumatized individuals are ashamed of things they've done—or things that have been done to them—to the point that they cannot imagine sharing the details with anyone, not even a trained therapist. Sometimes they are even afraid of what might change in their own emotional state if they finally fully acknowledge those experiences. They fear that the cap containing their unresolved, stored energy and emotion will break its seal, and they will lose control of their lives as a result.

Trained, experienced therapists hear shocking, tragic, even horrific stories from their patients. Through it all, their responsibility is to listen to a patient and help if possible, never judging. I don't always agree with the lifestyles and choices of my patients, yet I embrace each person I treat with an open mind and heart. If I busied myself with judgment, I would have little chance of helping anyone.

We can safely guess that everyone on the planet has judged someone at some point in their lives, so it is natural that patients would be wary of being judged by a therapist. But good therapists have a unique insight into the human condition that those in other professions don't always have; they understand why people behave in certain ways and what motivates them to do the things they do. When you know that unresolved pain motivates a person's actions, judgment doesn't come so easily.

Affordability can also be an obstacle for those seeking treatment. Many people know they need treatment. They want it. But they are certain they can't afford it. Countless people do not pursue psychological treatment because they are uneasy about the costs involved with therapy. When individuals are struggling financially, household budget cuts often leave treatment out of the picture, even though people in this situation are often more in need of immediate help than those under considerably less financial stress. If you are one of these people, take the time to research the costs and explore your options before giving up on treatment. You may be surprised at what you can afford. Talk to your health insurance company and inquire about mental health coverage. It may already be a part of your policy, even if you are unaware of it.

Some therapists may offer reduced or subsidized rates, payment plans, or some other method to help their patients with the cost. It may be, however, that your priorities need to be rearranged. Affording treatment may mean that you need to sacrifice some other non-necessity to accommodate this important process in your budget. You wouldn't deny yourself necessary medical care if you were in serious need of it; you would *find* a solution. Psychological treatment can be just as indispensable as urgent medical care.

One more barrier to seeking treatment is unfamiliarity with the process; people don't know what it involves, and they aren't willing to find out. Trauma and pain can also render a person blind to her own circumstances and depth of desperation.

Knowing when and how to seek treatment can seem overwhelming to someone suffering from trauma symptoms, but, in fact, it's quite simple. Almost anyone can benefit from psychological treatment at some point in his or her life to stay healthy and on track. Life can be very creative in the challenges it presents, and most people need help to overcome such challenges. If the question "Do I need therapy?" has ever arisen, there is a great chance that treatment could be very beneficial to you. Trauma has a way of finding nearly every person at some stage in life, and psychological treatment may be the only way to fully restore physical and emotional health in its wake.

"When should I seek treatment?" (Or, more likely, "When do I absolutely have to seek treatment?") The choice is yours, but we know that the sooner a victim of trauma can begin treatment, the better off the person will be. Early treatment can prevent the physiological symptoms of trauma from taking such a firm hold in the patient's mind and body. Again, however, we don't always have the awareness that a traumatic event has happened. We may not recognize or accept a certain event as having been traumatic. Or, we may not remember that it took place at all. In these instances, getting treatment soon after the event is impossible, so exploring the possibility of past trauma as a source of present difficulties is worth looking into. Ultimately, the success of your treatment may be determined by how committed you are to your own healing and your willingness to participate in the treatment process. You must have the courage to share the details of your life fully to allow your therapist to do his or her job well.

As stated earlier, almost everyone can benefit from psychological treatment. It is uncommon for a patient to regret the decision to seek therapy.

Making the Decision

Be honest with yourself about the challenges you are facing in your life.

- Do you struggle to maintain healthy relationships?

- Are you prone to addiction or substance abuse? Do you have self-esteem issues, depression, or anxiety?

- Do you have unexplained health issues such as insomnia, asthma, ulcers, migraines, seizures, or other health concerns?

Discovering trauma is similar to solving any mystery—there is no detail too small or insignificant to ignore. When reading about the potential symptoms of trauma (many symptoms are described in chapter 1 and in examples throughout the book), notice what strikes a chord for you, what sounds or feels familiar to you. If any of the classic trauma symptoms apply, I encourage you to consider treatment. There's no reason to live with these issues if you don't have to, and psychological treatment may be the only way to put them behind you.

As many of you have no doubt discovered, trauma doesn't end with you. Anyone who cares about you—spouse, parent, child, or friend—has been affected by your experience of trauma. Family members may also need therapy. Other treatment may be necessary to mend broken relationships. *If* other people in your life are ready to get therapy, that's wonderful. If they are not, however, your willingness to move forward with your own healing may be the inspiration they need to get help. Don't arrest your progress because other people in your life are putting on the brakes. It's easy for us to say that our spouse, our son, or our mother is the one who needs help, or that things will never get better unless both or all of you get help. When you're ready to commit to the help you need, you have to seize the moment and hope that others will follow. There's no time like *now*, regardless of the other circumstances in your life.

Once you make the decision to seek treatment, you have taken a tremendous step in the right direction. Sadly, many people never get to this point. The road to the final decision to get help is a long, arduous, and conflicting one. Once you make this difficult choice, entrusting your mental and emotional recovery to a professional can raise some challenges.

Finding a psychotherapist who fits you and your needs is important. There are thousands of professionals in this field, and not all of them are great at what they do, which is normal in any industry. Not all teachers are good teachers. Not all doctors are good doctors. Not all mechanics are good mechanics. You may be tempted to make an appointment with the first therapist you find. Depending on your situation, urgent care may be required. If you feel you need to see a professional and do not have the luxury of waiting for the perfect therapist to come your way, by all means, follow your instinct. If you can safely wait to make an appointment until you have thoroughly researched potential therapists and their approaches to treatment, your patience and diligence will no doubt prove beneficial in your search for an experienced, insightful therapist.

What Kind of Professional Am I Looking For?

First, it's important to understand the distinctions among mental health professionals. Different professions within the field require specific credentials, training, and specializations. They also differ considerably in the kind of treatment they can offer their patients; yet, the terms that describe their different roles are often used interchangeably.

Psychiatrists, for example, are often confused with psychotherapists or psychologists. Psychiatrists are medical doctors who focus on mental illness and, because they are doctors of medicine as opposed to doctors of philosophy or psychology, they traditionally treat their patients' illnesses by prescribing medical treatments and prescription pharmaceuticals. While many psychiatrists are trained in traditional talk therapy methods, they often do not emphasize this in their treatments. Psychiatrists look primarily to chemical therapy for their patients; a psychologist may refer you to a psychiatrist if he or she feels that you need a prescription in order to address your mental health concerns. Generally speaking, however, psychologists are not licensed to prescribe medication.

An appointment with a psychiatrist will usually be short and to the point. Once you are diagnosed and prescribed medication, the doctor will usually request a return visit to find out how you're doing and may then make adjustments to your prescription based on the information revealed in a short interview with you.

My experience has taught me that chemical therapy alone is not appropriate treatment for trauma-related emotional and physical issues, yet more and more people look to pharmaceuticals for solutions. The medications most often prescribed merely numb the symptoms of trauma and dampen the energetic sensations felt by the patient; they do not resolve the lasting effects of the trauma itself. Sadly, patients who adopt a chemical approach to their therapy may never truly find freedom from their problems, and when and if they ever stop taking the medication, their symptoms can return manyfold. They can end up in worse condition than they were when they began treatment. Drugs may deliver what seem to be extraordinary results, but their use comes with a price. Many prescription drugs have a substantial list of side effects that are not fully investigated before these medications find their way to the shelves. Many of them are highly addictive and easily abused by their users. Others are highly effective at first, but their effectiveness wanes, at which point the patient is switched to a new combination of drugs. In a years-long quest for relief, a patient can change medications dozens of times. In the process, the symptoms they are trying to relinquish (or avoid) return.

This isn't breaking news. Hundreds of people have attempted to expose the more dangerous, questionable practices of the pharmaceutical industry, but in spite of growing awareness about what motivates the sale and research of these drugs, Americans, in particular, cling to them fervently. We *want* happiness in a pill. Happiness doesn't come in a pill, but that doesn't keep us from trying to find it there. It has been my observation over the years that anyone who has a great quality of life—fulfillment, peace, and healthy relationships—works for it.

There is a time and a place for chemical therapy when treating trauma, but prescription drugs offer, at best, a short-term solution. I would never discourage someone in a high-risk situation—in danger of harming themselves or others—from accepting a prescribed chemical intervention. Rather, I suggest that once stability has been achieved, patients move away from chemical therapy and replace it with psychotherapy. Some specific disorders will require ongoing medication for patients to participate in psychotherapy sessions. However, it is my position that when a patient is able to abstain from chemical therapy or mind-altering substances of any kind, the healing of trauma is accelerated.

If a patient is self-medicating through addiction or drug abuse, or is taking prescribed medication beyond the intended amount or length of time for their trauma symptoms, we have little chance of helping them. These chemicals seem to quarantine the residual energy from the trauma, which psychotherapists need to access and mobilize in order to start the healing process.

Imagine a bottle of soda that you accidentally drop on the floor. If you unscrew the cap, the soda will, inevitably, explode sugary fizz all over the place the moment you break the seal. Our instinctive reaction in this situation is to tighten the cap again as soon as possible. If trauma is the pressurized air in the soda bottle, prescription drugs are the cap. You can't release the pressure without removing the cap, and if you do suddenly remove the cap, you'll make a mess. Chemical therapy may temporarily prevent the mess caused by trauma, but it does not treat the source of suffering—the traumatic experience.

If we continue the terms of our sugar-water metaphor, psychotherapy is the *gradual* turning of the cap. The slow release of the pressure creates a lasting solution to the problem. Psychologists and psychotherapists often use this approach.

An appointment with a psychotherapist differs greatly from an appointment with a typical psychiatrist. A psychotherapist engages his or her patients in carefully choreographed conversations about the patient's symptoms, experiences, and memories. The patient is not likely to receive a prescription from the doctor at the end of the visit because psychotherapists are not usually licensed to prescribe medicines.

Social workers and counselors are valuable players in the psychology field. They can offer counseling, empathy, advice, and coaching for patients on how to deal with relationships, communication, or personal struggles. They can counsel individuals dealing with stress, addiction, relationships problems, and countless other issues. I have found, however, that they are not ideal professionals to handle patients with acute trauma symptoms. Few have the tools and training to potentially heal the unresolved trauma that so many people suffer from. Most patients require specialized, intensive clinical therapy to overcome a traumatic history.

Finding a psychotherapist can be challenging. After a few unsuccessful visits with a professional, some patients lose enthusiasm for the process. In reality, pain can surface initially as a result of therapy, and patients may wrongly attribute this to the therapist. To avoid facing their pain, they may move from one therapist to another and never really start the process of healing.

In an ocean of psychotherapists, how do you know which one is right for you? In addition to credentials and doctoral degrees from accredited universities, you want a psychotherapist who specializes in areas that apply to your circumstances. Seeking a psychotherapist with a specialization or extensive experience with trauma and RMFR is, in my opinion, ideal. Remember, even if you don't see the connection between your symptoms and possibly traumatic events, a professional who is well versed in trauma treatment can make that connection for you.

Also, find out whether the professionals you are considering have been through therapy themselves. A quality therapist will have continued to seek individual therapy beyond the requirements of his schooling. This shows initiative and passion for the field and for his personal growth. If he has not been through extended therapy, his ability to provide effective, quality care could be dubious. A therapist who has not experienced an effective form of therapy as a patient may bring his or her own unresolved issues into your therapy session, which inevitably undermines the success of your treatment. Without the benefit of their own emotional and psychological fitness, they may be uncomfortable dealing with your experiences, which can trigger their own traumas and cause them to shy away from aggressively dealing with yours in treatment. As a therapist who has experienced incredible results through treatment, I question any professional who has not had some personal experience as a patient of the treatment they are providing. The therapist's willingness to confront his own history through treatment demonstrates his commitment to the healing process and to being the most capable psychotherapist he can be. The therapist who is actively pursuing his or her own healing in this way obviously believes in the power of his or her work. Therapists who have experienced hardship and the healing process will be more effective in treating you; their personal experiences will likely add to their abilities as therapists.

You also want to look for character and integrity in a therapist. If they don't follow the principles of their training and discipline, if they don't follow a strong code of ethics, you want to know this up front. Do your research, and don't compromise on these points. Ask friends and family for referrals; do research online. If your psychologist has any malpractice suits against him, you may want to keep looking. You must feel that your therapist is a stable person, someone you can trust to provide the stability necessary when things fall apart. This "falling apart" is a natural part of the process, and a good therapist will set the boundaries necessary to make you feel safe in this situation. Your therapist will ground you in reality when terror arises and will offer encouragement when it gets difficult—and, in most cases, it will get difficult. Old wounds and mistrust will come up; an experienced therapist expects this and will help you navigate this difficult territory. He will offer support if you're inclined to cut and run or give up in discouragement. If you feel that you and the therapist are mismatched, try to be rigorously honest with yourself about your own likely distrust. Talk about your misgivings openly. Note that trust and faith have been severely damaged in most victims of trauma. A good therapist will help you restore and rebuild these crucial capabilities. *You only need enough trust to get started.*

Your Part in the Process

Once you have chosen a therapist and begin working with him or her, it is vital that you commit to your healing and to the therapist you've chosen if you want your therapy to be successful. It's essential that you take responsibility for your own treatment. Your willingness to face difficult memories, feelings, and emotions will determine the momentum and effectiveness of your treatment plan. A component of this commitment is the willingness to be vulnerable—a tall order for anyone who has consciously or unconsciously armored himself to prevent feeling vulnerable. As we mentioned at the start of this book, working through the fear, shame, rage, and a multitude of other feelings that arise with a therapist takes a tremendous amount of courage. If you are able to summon that courage, you will reach the other side—a place where you have a new repertoire of responses to stressful situations in your life—and will be able to repair and restore your relationships with others.

How Long Will It Take?

Initially, your therapist will ask you what your expectations are, and the two of you will discuss the process. In many cases, the length of treatment depends on how long the experience of trauma has been entrenched. The healing of developmental trauma often takes longer. Shock trauma, trauma caused by grief, or a frightening one-time event can usually be healed more quickly.

Six weeks to two months would be considered short-term therapy and may be enough time to deal with certain traumatic issues. Weekly or biweekly (twice per week) treatment is often recommended. Those with more severe symptoms may be able to be restored to a level of functioning with brief therapy such as this, but true emotional health will take longer.

Even brief therapy with a therapist skilled in healing body and mind can restore the *desire* for emotional health and, in some cases, the desire for life itself. From this springboard, a return to experiencing the pleasure, joy, and love that life has to offer can begin.

CHAPTER 7

A Note to Veterans and Their Loved Ones

War has changed. Modern warfare is a high-tech operation. This means that today's service members are having a very different wartime experience than those who served forty years ago. They engage the enemy using sophisticated strategies, weapons, and procedures. They struggle to identify the enemies among the civilians. We have the technology to better protect our military. As a result, fewer US combat troops lose their lives, and more troops return home to their families.

There are, however, elements of war that will never change, regardless of time and technology. Most service members' lives are at risk. They often see and do horrific things, even if it simply means pushing a button. They watch their friends die. They are constantly aware of their dangerous circumstances. And they are put in situations where they must kill or be killed. In this way, Operation Iraqi Freedom (OIF) and Operation Enduring Freedom (OEF) are no different from any other war in history. Yet there are aspects of these wars that have significantly increased the likelihood of invisible wounds.

Since the first troops returned from Afghanistan and Iraq, studies and surveys have shown that approximately 15–20% of these veterans have psychological wounds. Many researchers predict that the real numbers are much higher. My professional experience makes me suspect that nearly every returned soldier harbors some trace of residual trauma from his wartime experience. Some will resolve their traumas. Many will not. The reality of over two million troops returning home in this condition in the coming years is overwhelming and one of the biggest challenges we face as this conflict continues. All of us will feel the shock waves.

Trauma and its psychological wounds often destroy relationships, families, and communities, even claiming lives. Everyone can be affected by a vet's trauma in personal, relational, social, and economical ways. Everyone benefits if vets get the treatment they need sooner rather than later.

The physical and emotional rehabilitation of our military is the key to preserving the future of our armed forces. While the wounds may lie underneath the surface, they can eventually rise to the top. When that happens, these men and women become dysfunctional, either in the field or in the world. Invisible wounds decrease a soldier's potential for a successful military career. These wounds diminish their ability to have functional, healthy relationships and reestablish their place in society. I believe it is our duty and our responsibility to ensure that these men and women receive the care needed to restore their emotional and psychological health. Without it, they may become casualties of this war even though they have physically survived it.

Why This War Is Different

A war we all hoped would be brief has continued since 2003. This conflict has employed a method of recycling troops that has greatly affected their ability to maintain emotional well-being and receive sufficient leave for psychological and emotional recovery. Deployments have been longer, and redeployment has been common. Dwell time between tours has been brief. Just as soldiers begin to adjust to normal life, they are called up again.

For example, a patient of ours did three tours in Iraq. During Brandon's first leave, he struggled with bouts of rage and could not connect with his family and friends as he once had. He found their conversations and complaints about civilian life tedious and irritating. He was anxious to go back. A month later, he was redeployed. With each deployment, Brandon's transition to civilian life became more and more difficult and compounded the effects of his psychological wounds.

Many service members can identify with Brandon's experience as they return home with visible and invisible wounds. Although this is a high-tech war, it is still a violent one. Improvised explosive devices (IEDs) are a constant threat and have led to service members losing limbs or suffering traumatic brain injuries (TBIs). Many soldiers have been maimed or killed, and many who survived are traumatized because they witnessed these tragedies. As we have learned, it is very common for emotional trauma to accompany physical injuries.

The threat of violence or attack is enough to traumatize even the most disciplined soldier. And the possibility of being wounded or killed or of killing another human being leads to a state of constant hyper-vigilance. This is known as "Terrorist Trauma Syndrome" or TTS, a term coined by Dr. David Fair. Some soldiers may never fire a gun during their tour but will suffer psychological wounds due to TTS and the effects of prolonged hyper-vigilance. They pass time waiting for the possibility (or even the opportunity) for violence. Due to the constant threat of danger, they are in the first stages of the stress response at all times.

In our post-9-11 world, TTS sometimes affects civilians as well. Color-coded threat level indicators, strict air travel policies, and hyper-focused media attention on the state of terrorism leave us constantly aware of a possible terrorist attack. The threat of danger has traumatized many more Americans than were in New

York on that tragic day. But troops in Afghanistan and Iraq face these dangers at close range.

Many service members and their families also become "secondary" trauma victims. Secondary trauma—stress resulting from helping or wanting to help a traumatized or suffering person—is very common among psychotherapists, psychologists, and other mental health professionals as well as among emergency workers (EMTs, physicians, fire, police, search and rescue, etc.) who are continually exposed to the suffering of others. But the risk for secondary trauma is not limited to professions in which such exposure is common. Loved ones of returned service members can become secondary trauma victims as they try to cope with their family member's psychological and physical wounds.

All these factors contribute to the skyrocketing rates of psychological wounding resulting from the conflicts in Iraq and Afghanistan.

Defining Psychological Wounds

Anyone can have psychological wounds, or emotional trauma, but veterans nearly always suffer from psychological damage as well as physical injuries, such as TBIs or loss of limbs. The physical wounds of war combined with the experiences of combat can lead to severe emotional trauma. In the context of the military, trauma and its symptoms are often referred to as post-traumatic stress disorder, or PTSD.

PTSD has been attached to the veteran experience since the Vietnam War. The condition had different labels before it became known as PTSD, but it wasn't until after that war that we began to truly understand it. Today, the term is used to describe acute or chronic emotional, psychological, and physiological responses to traumatic events. Soldiers aren't the only people affected by

PTSD. The psychological and physiological processes that cause PTSD are the same in any individual who experiences trauma, but a soldier's experience is unmatched.

The nature of war creates a shared experience among veterans. They encounter a range of potentially traumatic events on a daily basis that would be devastating to a civilian in a single occurrence. They are trained to always be aware of threats and their surroundings. In technical terms, they are always hyper-alert, which is the high-intensity state that leads to being traumatized.

To help them deal with these experiences in the moment, soldiers are conditioned for detachment. They are told to think of themselves as if they are already dead. This enables them to carry out difficult orders in high-stress situations and cope with their environment. Many soldiers describe it as "numbness." However, that numbness begins to wear off when they return home, and they start to feel the pain associated with the things they've seen and done, as in a delayed reaction.

Brandon experienced this rather painful transition between tours. He had to live in a desensitized psychological state in Iraq. It was the only way he could function in that environment, an environment full of danger and uncertainty. The numbness was an aspect of his training that enabled him to carry out orders in spite of circumstances. Brandon had to be numb to keep going when each day in front of him could easily be his last.

But when he was home, the numbness began to wear off. He began to feel the emotional and physical pain of his experiences. Without the tools to successfully confront those feelings and learn to interact with his civilian family and friends, the feelings were completely overwhelming. The symptoms of his trauma were so intense that they were unbearable. Many service members, such as Brandon, feel that the only way to find relief is to be numb again.

Common Symptoms of PTSD

Many veterans experience acute trauma symptoms once they return home. It may take several weeks or months for them to recognize their feelings and emotions. For others, it may take a few days.

Symptoms of PTSD can be physical as well as emotional. Moderate to severe depression is extremely common among veterans. They feel guilty—about things they did or because they survived when others did not. They feel isolated by their experiences, and they struggle to identify with anyone other than fellow military personnel. But the symptoms don't end there. Between emotional, physiological, and behavioral symptoms, the list of possibilities is almost limitless.

Symptoms of PTSD may include the following:

Fatigue

Poor digestion, poor appetite

Unexplained illness

Distorted speech patterns

Insomnia

Muscle pain

General pain

Headaches

Cold hands and feet

Increased heart rate

Immune deficiency

Nausea

Dizziness

Fidgeting, restlessness

Sexual dysfunction

Excessive sweating

Intrusive memories and flashbacks

Memory loss, amnesia

Withdrawal, feelings of detachment

Lack of emotion

Anxiety

Confusion

Outbursts of anger, rage

Aggression

Low self-esteem, low confidence

Paranoia

Confusion

Difficulty concentrating

Lack of focus

Depression

Irritability

Suicidal thoughts

Depending on the nature of their experience and the severity of the trauma, veterans have varying reactions to wartime events. Some may be quite functional with only a few mild symptoms. In fact, they may feel they can cope with the symptoms on their own and don't need treatment. Others can be quite troubled and symptomatic to the point that they become violent or suicidal.

It is very important that friends and family of veterans closely observe their loved ones. Many veterans will insist they are fine, but such may not be the case. Pay close attention to their behaviors, and you may be able to intervene before trauma leads to tragedy. Veterans need help to heal their traumas, just like the rest of us. They are not super-human. More about trauma danger signals and first aid appears in the following chapter; however, as with other types of trauma victims, some common warning signs in veterans' behavior include addiction and reenactment.

Veterans and Addiction

Whatever their symptoms, it is common for veterans to self-medicate. Addiction is widespread among veterans, and alcohol or drug use can set in just days after they return home. What starts as a need to decompress, have fun, and "make up for lost time" can turn into a full-blown addiction in a short time. In fact, many veterans resort to using drugs or alcohol on a daily basis.

Veterans often turn to drugs and alcohol because they want to numb symptoms of trauma. These substances keep the feelings and memories at bay. Their symptoms return when the high wears off, however, and the need to alleviate these symptoms creates an addictive pattern. It isn't accurate to say that they want to abuse drugs and alcohol. Rather, the issue is that they will do anything to feel "normal" again, or at least, comfortably numb. The same is true for almost any traumatized individual with a substance abuse problem.

Substance issues in veterans should be taken very seriously because they can escalate quickly. I treated a veteran of OIF who drank a gallon of vodka per day at the peak of his alcoholism. During the same time, he was involved in a severe accident while driving under the influence. It nearly killed him.

A veteran doesn't have to drink a gallon of vodka a day to indicate he is troubled by his experiences. Simply drinking more than usual could be enough. If you notice these behaviors, you may want to encourage your loved one to seek help.

Addiction also fuels the self-destructive behaviors often exhibited by veterans. Many veterans engage in risky behaviors, such as reckless driving or other high-speed, thrill-seeking activities. They may do things that are clearly dangerous, such as drinking and driving or consuming quantities of drugs and alcohol that could be fatal. For example, a young soldier in my community returned home from his first tour in Iraq back in 2003. His family was so relieved to have him safe at home, especially because he was only twenty years old. One month after his return, the young man was killed in an accident. He was driving an all-terrain vehicle that flipped, crushing him underneath. His friends said he kept going faster, turning harder, and taking chances he would not have taken before.

His family was shocked and devastated. But his story is not uncommon. Veterans often feel detached from the risk involved with certain behaviors because they are disconnected from feelings of fear and anxiety. They may feel bulletproof or think that rules no longer apply to them.

Some service members feel guilty that they survived while their comrades fell. This "survivor's guilt" can also lead to high-risk behavior. Many of these survivors are unable to identify the risks associated with certain activities because their judgment is skewed as a result of shame or regret.

When individuals are in a state of hyper-vigilance for long periods of time, the rational brain often becomes irrational. This scenario is especially true for service members whose traumatic situations can last for months at a time. Tours are long, and threats can occur on a daily basis. At the end of the day, they don't get to go home and recuperate. They have to get up and do it all over again the next day. Over time, a person's ability to evaluate risk becomes impaired, and he can carry that impairment home when the tour is over.

Veterans and Reenactment

Reckless behavior can also be a form of reenactment, a common reaction to trauma, especially in veterans. Because military troops are often still in a state of hyper-awareness when they return home, the activity that surrounds them seems to move very slowly compared to the storm of energy brewing inside them. They may crave speed, risk, and danger because these are the only things they can feel through their numbness. Many of the experiences they seek out mimic the scenarios that traumatized them in the first place. One service member who came to us for help regularly dove into the depths of dark caves beneath the sea in Hawaii, an extremely dangerous undertaking. He craved the excitement, and he became addicted to the thrill.

Traumatized individuals often unconsciously seek out situations that mirror their traumatic event because of their deep physiological and psychological need to complete the stress response. However, these efforts rarely lead to success and often leave the individual physically wounded, in trouble in his relationships or with authorities, or re-traumatized.

For example, Ray was deployed to Afghanistan, and while he was there, he accidentally killed a civilian man. He was horrified by what he had done and felt overwhelmed by guilt. But, despite the fact that his killing another human being was a traumatizing event, he nearly killed another man a few months after he returned home. An argument with his brother turned physical, and Ray became so enraged and out of control that he nearly beat his own brother to death.

During his tour, Ray was forced to confront one of his deepest fears: taking someone's life. Because he was traumatized by that experience, he is repeatedly drawn to intense conflicts that often turn violent. He is drawn to them because he unconsciously believes that it is the only way to find relief from his trauma. The stress response described in the first three chapters of this book is desperately trying to complete its cycle and release the tremendous pressure in Ray's mind and body that is trapped beneath the surface of consciousness.

The Stigma of PTSD

Post-traumatic stress disorder is just a name for a catalogue of symptoms that follow a stressful situation. Veterans are not the only people on earth with PTSD. Yet the term has a very negative connotation in the military world. Veterans often feel that a PTSD diagnosis reduces the uniqueness of their individual reactions, feelings, and struggles. Or they may feel stigmatized, labeled, and devalued by their peers.

In truth, veterans experience a wide range of reactions following deployment, and the symptoms can be minor or severe. Instead of using this name as a label, it is important to reestablish post-traumatic stress disorder as merely a collection of possible symptoms caused by trauma. It is not limited to war veterans, and those suffering from PTSD may not be permanently damaged; they can heal with proper treatment. Unfortunately, many vets can't or won't pursue therapy.

Treating wounds that are invisible to the eye is challenging. But it isn't the challenge of healing that dissuades vets from getting the help they need. Many of them don't want help, don't know they need help, or are afraid to get help. Codes of respect and honor are integral to our military structure, and the culture of this group is the glue that holds it together. Service members who sense they've had an emotional reaction to their experiences are reluctant to come forward because they might lose the respect of their peers or superiors. They are afraid they will be considered weak, and, given the culture of the military, they're not entirely off point. These veterans would rather suffer in silence than risk losing their rank or job, pride, reputation, or image. Losing face with fellow vets or letting themselves down is an option too costly for many.

It can also be very difficult for soldiers to recognize their wounds in a military atmosphere. During deployment or training, they are in a mind-set that is necessary for their survival. Similar experiences and wounds burden their peers. For many service members, it isn't until they return to civilian life (even temporarily) with their family and friends that their psychological wounds become apparent. Suddenly, they feel like fish out of water gasping for air.

Many veterans who reach that point, however, do not seek help. Once they get home, they are ready to make up for lost time. They want to spend time with their families and start living again, which is why the military's post-deployment mental health survey is often ignored, or the problems reported are minimized. Service members say they feel fine to avoid being detained for evaluation. Instead, they go directly home. More often than not, sadly, their experiences eventually catch up with them.

Treatment Options for Veterans

Soldiers who do look to the military for help often receive insufficient treatment, in spite of the dedicated efforts of many VA treatment personnel. The military's approach to dealing with PTSD and psychological wounds emphasizes chemical therapy. While pharmaceutical drugs can provide a quick, short-term fix in extreme situations, they are not the long-term solution to this problem. Many drugs prescribed to veterans have harsh side effects, which can be as debilitating as their trauma symptoms. And if veterans ever stop taking their medications, their symptoms often return, bringing them back to square one.

What does proper treatment look like? The US Department of Veterans' Affairs (VA) and The Department of Defense (DOD) cannot meet the needs of all the service members returning home. There are just too many of them. The standardized approach of these organizations cannot provide complete healing for the service members and veterans with the most severe psychological wounds. As the government works to revamp its systems, many veterans will miss out on the treatment they need unless they look to other sources for help, such as private psychotherapy practices and programs specializing in trauma.

All Americans can and will be affected by veterans with invisible wounds. Unresolved concealed wounds pose a major threat to our armed forces, to their families, and to our economy. If trauma symptoms are unaddressed, traumatized service members will end up needing longer-term care or treatment, whether it is therapy, medication, or medical care, and regardless of whether it is effective. There may be other associated costs to society, as well. Timely, effective trauma treatment is the best way to reduce the lasting impact of war in this country socially, economically, and individually. It is the best way for these dedicated men and women to take back the lives they so bravely risked for all of us.

Understanding trauma in veterans, a significant group in our population, illuminates how trauma affects our society as well as each individual. Trauma can derail a life. It can destroy a family. And it can influence an entire nation. Training, psychological fortitude, and bravery cannot prevent the effects of trauma, even in the most skilled and decorated soldiers. The repercussions can be as debilitating as a physical wound and as worthy of a Purple Heart as other demonstrations of valor. Let us respect our armed forces for their sacrifices and remember that their battle continues long after they come home. They deserve to be on the frontlines of healing trauma in body, mind, and spirit.

CHAPTER 8

Danger Signals and Trauma First Aid

There are things you can do for yourself and others to aid recovery in the first moments, days, and months after a traumatic experience. Timely interventions can prevent symptoms from taking a stronger hold in our minds and bodies and can prevent years of pain and confusion. You don't have to be a psychotherapist to perform trauma first aid any more than you must be a doctor to perform CPR. If you study the warning signs and learn helpful techniques, you may be able to save lives in the aftermath of trauma; you may be able to save your own.

Imagine that you encounter a friend, loved one, or even a stranger just moments after he or she has a traumatic experience—your child falls out of his favorite climbing tree, your best friend loses a parent, or you stop on the side of the road to help someone who's just been in an accident. All of these incidents are, or can be, deeply traumatic. Your actions during this very sensitive time can make a real difference to the person in need.

If someone other than you has just experienced trauma, do the following:

- First, introduce yourself and ask the person's name if you don't already know it.

81

- Let him know he is safe and secure. If necessary, find a quiet place away from the site of the incident.

- It is important that you ask his permission to interact. This is a good way to establish his ability to respond in the moment while showing respect for his fragile boundaries. Use simple dialogue, such as Do you mind if I sit with you? Can I speak with you? Is this OK? Are you ready (able, etc.) for the next step? If he is not ready to talk about the incident, don't persist. Instead, try focusing his attention on the present and ask him to talk about what he might be experiencing or feeling.

- Be gentle, supportive, and acknowledging of his fear or pain.

- When the victim appears more focused, you can engage him in a dialogue about his current experiences and about the event itself if the information is necessary. Again, let him know he is safe, and ask him to briefly describe what happened to him.

- It's important that you never criticize the way victims responded during the incident. If they ran away out of fear, put themselves in danger, or contributed to the incident, don't bring this to their attention at this time. You want them to feel comfortable talking to you about the details.

Allow them to indulge their physical and emotional responses to the event. If they start to cry, tremble, or become emotional, your words of encouragement can be the permission they need to express their feelings. Completing these physical and emotional stress responses will enable them to recover from the event more quickly and completely. Once they have stabilized from the initial aftermath of the experience, they can begin to process the details of the event itself.

If the traumatic incident is one that requires medical or legal involvement, such as police or paramedics, be aware that their entry into the scene can further traumatize the individual. Be an advocate for your friend or loved one even while the first response team does its job. Law enforcement personnel may feel compelled to question and press the victim about the details of the event before he is ready. If the individual is not in a psychological state that allows him to discuss these things, this step can interrupt the winding down (completion) of the stress response, leaving the victim more vulnerable to the effects of trauma.

Again, allow victims to talk through their feelings and experience pain about the event. Don't tell them not to cry or that they shouldn't have certain feelings. Also, don't shy away from conversations and questions about God, faith, forgiveness, or anger. Victims of a traumatic event often need to understand why it happened and what it means, and you can help them explore these important questions. It may not be wise to impose your own religious or spiritual values on a victim unless he or she is like-minded, however. *Listening* is more important.

After the initial event, encourage the individual to seek the help of a trained psychotherapist even before symptoms begin to emerge. Many people desperately want to return to their lives as they were before the traumatic experience and will deny the severity or intensity of the event. Be supportive and nonjudgmental in your campaign for their healing. Try not to pressure the victim with your own agenda, but strongly encourage them in the direction of seeking appropriate help. Be empathetic and compassionate, and use your objective observations. Explain that their pain is likely to get worse with time and that qualified help can assist in getting their lives back on track.

Your Reaction to Another's Trauma

Your reactions can also interrupt a victim's winding down process. You don't want to burden a trauma victim with your own feelings or cause further panic. Try to stay calm if you can. If you sense you aren't in a balanced state, take note of what you're feeling or experiencing. Your bodily sensations can be clues about your response to the situation. For example, shortness of breath, tensing muscles, and accelerated heart rate can be signs of hyper-arousal. This is a normal reaction to a high-stress situation and *you* will need to take steps to wind down from this state later, and as soon after the event as possible. Otherwise, you can become a secondary trauma victim. In the meantime, you will need to push the "pause button." The pause button allows you to put your feelings and sensations on hold so you can help the victim; you will be able to resolve them later.

Here are two suggestions to assist you in *pausing* to help the victim:

- You can diffuse your hyper-aroused state by taking deep breaths. Concentrate on your breathing and think about slowing down.

- Focus on thinking and moving slowly. This should help to clear your head and calm your nerves so you can then redirect your attention back to the victim.

As I have discovered through personal experience, helping others deal with trauma can be very rewarding, but it is important to help yourself after assisting someone to cope with a traumatic experience. Having a strong network of friends and family is extremely valuable in this situation, and there are practical things you can do for yourself as well, to help you cope with the emotional and physical symptoms of what is sometimes called "secondary" trauma.

Because trauma is a physiological as well as an emotional experience, it is important at this time to take care of your body. When your physical body is healthy, it can recover from trauma more quickly and completely. For example:

- Eat regular, healthy, nutritious meals even if you don't feel hungry.

- Get lots of rest.

- Relieve stress symptoms with regular exercise.

- Avoid caffeine, as it can interfere with sleep patterns.

- Don't use drugs or alcohol. Even prescription and over-the-counter drugs can complicate your healing process.

In my opinion, these are things we should do every day, regardless of challenging circumstances. But in the aftermath of a traumatic event, taking exceptional care of your body can expedite your recovery.

You will want to take steps and create systems to help you reestablish your emotional stability as well. After trauma, everything can seem upside down and out of place. You can feel uncomfortable in your own skin, and daily activities can be a struggle. Be deliberate in your efforts to regain a sense of normalcy. For example:

- Maintain your usual routine, but don't push yourself to do extra tasks.

- Structure your time and set small goals and priorities.

- Make as many small daily decisions as possible—what to make for dinner, for example—as this can help you regain your sense of control.

- Avoid making any major life changes or decisions.

Whether you are the victim of trauma or you are helping a victim of trauma, the most important step in your recovery process is allowing yourself to feel differently after a traumatic event without denying or ignoring your feelings. Many trauma victims don't know what to do with the feelings they have after such an experience, so they ignore them or pretend they don't exist. In the long run, this can do significant harm. If you have recurring thoughts about the event, don't try to avoid them. They are a normal part of the process. Don't beat yourself up because you feel bad about the experience when you think you shouldn't. Give yourself permission to feel the way you feel.

Share your feelings with others, and talk to people you trust. You might be surprised at how many people want to help and support you. At the same time, you may need to set limits with your support system when you don't feel like talking. Journaling can be another outlet for your feelings.

Also, make a point to do things you enjoy. After a traumatic event, you may need to create positive experiences for yourself. Watch your favorite movie, go out to dinner, or read a book. The point is not to simply stay busy, which can be an avoidance mechanism, but rather to make a conscious effort to seek out pleasurable situations.

If you have a relationship with the victim that extends beyond the incident (friends or family), you can continue to help her recover from her traumatic experience by reaffirming her hopes for the future and guiding her toward resources and behavior that promote healing. Be a positive voice that paints an optimistic view of the future. Victims often blame themselves for the event or have guilt about their actions. Thoughts like these can lead to more advanced symptoms of trauma, such as depression, guilt, or shame. Counter such thoughts with positive affirmation. Remind the victim that she "did the right thing," or "did nothing wrong," or that "everyone makes mistakes," whichever is most appropriate.

And, whether you are a victim of trauma or are trying to help someone who is, don't be afraid to seek professional help. Coping with trauma on your own in either case can be a very painful process. Refusing help can suspend, delay, or undermine your recovery. Having the courage to accept help can and does accelerate the healing process. Take care of yourself so that you can take care of others.

Helping Children Deal with Trauma

You can apply similar trauma first aid when working with children, but you may need to be even more sensitive regarding their emotional state about the event. The most important thing you can do for a child after a traumatic experience is to listen. Children may need to talk about the event and talk about it often. It may seem that they talk about the event excessively, but it is essential that they be allowed to fully express their fears and worries about the experience. Be supportive, sympathetic and attentive, but don't overreact. Other children may refuse to talk about the incident at all and may need to be drawn out of their protective shell by a parent, relative, friend, or professional therapist.

Also, don't feel like you need to "fix it" for them. Let them know that their feelings are normal, and show that you accept and embrace their feelings. A child will feel safe in general (and not just in regard to traumatic events) when she can talk freely about her feelings without judgment, teasing, or being told she should feel differently. Help her to integrate the experience. Acknowledge that things are not, or may not be, the same as before the incident, while offering hope and healing in the future.

Feeling safe is an important part of establishing a new "normal" for a child after such an experience.

Focus on facts while helping children cope with trauma. Ask them what they know about the event, and don't assume they understand exactly what happened. If they have questions about the experience, be as honest as possible. Many adults believe they should protect children from the truth about certain situations. In reality, children want as much concrete information as they can get. Share as much factual information as you can, based on the child's age and maturity level.

Also, don't sugarcoat these facts. Adults avoid direct conversations with children about troubling events by using euphemisms. For example, they say a loved one "went to sleep" or "went away" instead of saying that he died. Statements such as these can do more harm than good in the long run; they leave the child in limbo, waiting for the loved one to return. Divorce or the departure of a parent can also be tempting circumstances in which to gloss over the facts. For example, in the film *Forrest Gump,* Forrest's mother explains his father's absence by saying he's "on vacation." It's a humorous example, and not a wise one to follow. Parents often feel the need to spare their children from the truth, but in difficult circumstances, it's best to be as forthcoming as possible.

Some parents have trouble speaking in concrete terms with their children because they are struggling with the event themselves. It may be difficult for them to accept the death of that loved one or the consequences of life transitions. As a parent, you must be in tune with your own fears and feelings when responding to your children after a traumatic incident. Otherwise, you may transfer your own fears to your child and hinder their ability to heal from the experience. For example, if the event in question posed a threat to your child's health or safety, it can be as traumatic for you as the parent as it was for the child. You might feel an increased need to protect your child and experience anxiety if separated from him, even when he is at school. As adults, it is our responsibility to take care of our own fears; we cannot expect our children to do it for us. Dramatic changes in you or in the home after a traumatic event can magnify a child's fractured sense of safety. If you're having trouble dealing with the incident, find help to cope with your own fears.

In the months following a critical incident, you must be in tune to your child's needs and behaviors, and you may need to make allowances. Here are some additional actions to take in order to help your child or teen cope with trauma:

- Spend extra time together, have fun, do things as a family.
- Respect their privacy, especially with teens.
- Allow older children time away from family to process their experiences with their peers.
- Be prepared to tolerate aggressive behaviors.
- Remember to give lots of affection and hugs.
- Reward good and responsible behavior.
- Reinforce for the child that the event was not his fault.
- Watch for reenactment in teens and repetitive play in children.
- Monitor violent play or artwork, as it can be a form of catharsis or a sign that things are getting worse.
- Expect nightmares or bad dreams.
- Make other people in the child's life aware of the event's effects (babysitters, teachers, friends, neighbors, etc.).
- Speak positively and hopefully about the future.
- Connect with trauma specialists if necessary.

Trauma first aid may not prevent an individual from being traumatized to some extent; certain events leave permanent marks on our minds and bodies no matter what is done. Taking these steps, however, can expedite healing and make it possible to recover more fully with the help of a trained psychotherapist or other professional trauma specialist. It may also prevent more severe symptoms from settling in through the years to come.

Unfortunately, we can't always be by someone's side moments after a life-altering experience, but when we understand the signs and symptoms of trauma, we may be able to lead those suffering from trauma to get the help they desperately want and need.

One of the most terrifying consequences of traumatic experience from the point of view of a parent, or any loved one, is the heightened risk of suicide faced by those who survive it.

Risk of Suicide

First, be observant when dealing with a traumatized individual. Loved ones of suicide victims often recognize too late that there were warning signs. Understand the possible warning signs of suicidal behavior. If you suspect a person may be contemplating suicide, trust your judgment.

Suicidal behavior results from many different traumatic experiences, from sexual abuse to a disabling accident to the death of a loved one. It can also be caused by seemingly less serious life situations that are uncontrollable, such as a successful professional's job loss or an exemplary student's experience of poor grades. As this book illustrates, almost anything can lead to trauma if the event is unexpected and the person has a negative reaction to the experience, particularly if she has suffered developmental trauma in childhood.

Look for specific, telltale behaviors in your loved one, such as the following:

- Crying and withdrawal

- Recklessness

- Quitting activities and lack of interest in former activities

- Loss of appetite

- Lack of interest in appearance

- Diminished physical energy

- Frequent minor illness

- Sadness, hopelessness, guilt, loneliness

- Scattered thoughts

- Drug or alcohol abuse

Pay special attention to any individual with a previous history of suicidal behavior or suicide attempts. And certainly, take action if someone close to you begins talking about suicide or shares plans of suicide. At this stage, professional help is absolutely necessary and should be sought as soon as possible. If you feel your loved one is at a very high risk of suicide, don't leave him alone; call help to the scene.

Drastically elevated moods after a long period of deep depression can also be a warning sign that a suicide attempt is imminent. Once a person has resolved to commit suicide, he or she may exhibit behaviors that seem almost euphoric. The shift is usually sudden and without any change in life circumstances. The change can distract loved ones and friends from the victim's condition, giving them hope that things are turning around. In fact, such a dramatic change in behavior is a smokescreen for the increasingly dark feelings and can be a sign that a suicide attempt is just days or even hours away.

Many family members of suicide victims wish their loved one had shared their despair and plans with them. If so, they feel they could have stopped it. But most people contemplating suicide keep their plans to themselves. Therefore, it's up to those around them to stay in tune with their behaviors. If you are suspicious, ask the other people in your circle what they have noticed.

Even if you aren't convinced that your loved one is contemplating suicide, reach out to her and show you care. Be open to hearing what she has to say, but also tell her what you have noticed in her behavior, referencing specific actions and incidents. Then, ask direct questions about her current state. Don't be afraid to say the word suicide. Talk to her about her plans, previous attempts, and thoughts about suicide, if applicable. Listen, talk openly, and let her talk. Try to be understanding and open-minded about her thought process and feelings. This is the time to determine her risk for suicide.

Most important, try not to become upset or over-emotional during these conversations. Becoming upset might discourage at-risk people from talking to you again about their situation, and you want to keep an open dialogue so you can continue to monitor them. By mitigating your reaction in this way, you *pause* your own feelings and emotions about the situation in the moment. Remember, you must deal with these emotions at some point, allowing yourself to experience your feelings when it's more appropriate. Ignoring your feelings indefinitely or overriding them for an extended period will only do you harm, and you will likely become a secondary trauma victim.

Finally, offer hope and solutions to those at risk. Discuss the option of seeking professional help to deal with their pain. If they are resistant, help them imagine what life could be like without pain and despair. Let them know that such a life is possible for them with the right help and support, including that of friends and family, and counselors and therapists. Resolve to find help for your at-risk loved ones even if they are resistant. Be firm and diligent about your intentions to get help for them, even if they refuse to get it for themselves. When the danger signals are present, don't wait for confirmation of their plans to seek professional help; move forward on your own if at all possible. (See chapter 6, "Seeking Treatment.") They might ask you to keep your conversation secret. Don't. Secrets can be deadly.

There is hope, and there is a solution. We have learned a lot about the effects of trauma in recent decades, and even more about the process of healing from it.

CHAPTER 9

Crises and Hard Times

As I write this book, we are experiencing a strange and historic time. The United States has been at war for more than a decade. Thousands of men and women have lost their lives in this conflict, and those who survive return home broken with little hope for repair. The US economy is the worst it has been in eighty years. Millions have lost their jobs, and hundreds of thousands more face foreclosure on their homes. And those who haven't are afraid that they will. People are scared. They fear what is to come. Worst of all, they feel powerless to change their circumstances.

To say that these are "hard times" diminishes the suffering and difficulty that many are going through. Many people have had their worst fears come true. They have no income but plenty of financial obligations. They may have lost their homes and moved in with relatives or friends. Or worse, they may have lost their homes and have nowhere to go.

Some have seen sons, daughters, or fathers and mothers deployed to Iraq or Afghanistan, only to learn that they are never coming home. Others don't know what to do about their returned service member's psychological wounds, and their family is unraveling as a result.

Things happen in the world that we cannot change or control. But because these moments are unavoidable, the traumatizing nature of such events is often erroneously dismissed. Financial hardship and drastic changes to a person's surroundings and situation can be emotionally and psychologically unsettling. Crises can arise in the form of financial adversity and familial conflict. Millions are struggling with what could ultimately be the most difficult years of their lives. If we want to emerge completely from this crisis—as individuals and as a nation—we must be willing to take care of each other and take control of our own emotional healing.

What Is a Crisis?

A crisis is different from the daily challenges of living. Crises are life-defining moments, periods, or stages. As opposed to the normal fears and anxieties that come up on any given day, they are unique. A crisis is an event that completely overwhelms us. It is terrifying. We spend every ounce of energy, every thought, every effort to ensure our survival. A crisis could also be called trauma. Most people in crisis mode engage the physiological stress response that we've talked about in this book.

During a financial crisis, we may feel that our livelihoods and identities are at stake. Life as we've known it has come to an end. And because hard times can last months, even years, people can easily become stuck in some phase of the stress response and become traumatized. As economies and societies recover from financial crises, so must people, both physically and emotionally. When we suffer financial crisis, we suffer psychological crisis as well.

Crises and Co-occurring Traumas

For those who harbor unresolved past traumas, crisis situations can be particularly challenging. Previously traumatized individuals most often feel the fear and anxiety during a crisis more intensely. When we enter stressful times in our lives, traumatic experiences from the past are often brought to the surface. Even if those events happened years, even decades, earlier, the unresolved energy and emotions from those experiences often intensify the emotions associated with our current circumstances. When we experience this, responding to our situation appropriately becomes even more difficult than usual. This is known as *co-occurring* trauma.

Potentially, these surfacing emotions and experiences can help us move forward in a crisis. Some people react to trauma with action, using the energy of the stress response to fuel activity. People still wounded and in need of healing but able to take action often fare better than those who become paralyzed when things get tough.

Prior traumas can also cause people to "check out" emotionally and psychologically when crises arise. In these instances, they may be stuck in the "freeze" portion of the stress response from prior trauma. Rather than working frantically to solve the problem at hand, these individuals will be paralyzed, absolutely unable to take action. They cannot do what needs to be done to create solutions. Unfortunately, a passive, paralytic response (or lack of response, as it were) can exacerbate their wounded physiological and psychological state, causing them to ignore the needs of their present situation. They are not more traumatized than a more proactive person in the same situation; they simply respond differently. I'll share an example.

Scott and Michelle came to my clinic looking to improve their marriage. Scott had lost his job several months earlier, and the bank foreclosed on their home shortly after that. Because they had no home, they were forced to return to Scott's hometown.

The small town where he grew up is haunting territory for Scott because it is the scene of a very traumatic childhood. Scott's developmental trauma combined with his combat experiences in Iraq left him emotionally and psychologically wounded. Now that his role as a provider is threatened by this financial downturn, he is following his usual pattern when faced with hardship. He appears emotionally detached and incapable of action. Instead of working alongside his wife to repair their finances, Scott seems impervious to their situation and lives out his days as if they do not have a crisis on their hands. He is in full "collapse."

His wife, Michelle, responds differently in crises. She feels panicked about their circumstances and is supporting Scott and their two small children on her own. She has her own history of trauma but habitually responds to crises with intense, emotion-driven activity.

Scott and Michelle both have traumatic pasts, but they respond to crises in dramatically different ways. This mismatch in their personalities is causing serious strain in their marriage during this life-altering period. They need to be a team now more than ever if they want to restore their financial standing and support each other emotionally. But past traumas coupled with their differing responses cause Scott and Michelle to react to each other and to recent events with drastic opposition.

Feeling Unarmed in a Crisis

Times of crisis reveal to us how human we really are—both the good and the bad aspects of our character. Socially acceptable behaviors and habits that dictate our daily functioning can fall by the wayside in crises, and basic instincts can take over. They can expose the more primitive side of our human nature, making a situation even more frightening than it already is. We can feel powerless, desperate, and out of control, and these emotions can perpetuate the problem.

When crisis situations bring out the worst in us, the exposure can be devastating. Many people become distraught seeing the worst sides of themselves and others. In the days and weeks following Hurricane Katrina, lawlessness took over New Orleans. It was every man for himself. The infrastructure of the city completely collapsed. But even in this chaos, hundreds of people seized the opportunity to help others. Survivors ventured out in their personal fishing boats to look for strangers in need of rescue. People dropped everything to drive across the country bringing food, water, and clothing. The crisis revealed extremes in good and bad human behavior.

Can we choose the way we respond to crisis? Difficult times *can* present tremendous opportunities to reveal the best parts of our nature. It does feel like we are swimming upstream at first, but if we approach crises, and prolonged hardship in particular, with a positive, responsible attitude, we will find it is easier to keep moving forward.

Keeping Our Wits in Hard Times

How can we respond positively in a crisis when our first instinct may be to hide under the covers? We may feel worthless and defeated. The pain of a crisis can convince us to believe these critical kinds of internal declarations. If we buy into such ideas, we risk retreating further into despair.

Remembering the lessons we have learned from past hardships and experiences can be extremely valuable in times of trial. Recognizing that the lessons we will learn from the present challenges will be highly beneficial to other areas of our lives is valuable as well. If we survived the past, we can survive the present. Life experiences—both traumatic and otherwise—prepare us for future challenges that we will be responsible to overcome. They help us develop survival mechanisms and coping skills. In a way, they are blessings in disguise.

When it comes to dealing with a crisis situation, rational thinking can be our life preserver. The "go-to" response may be panic, but this response rarely produces a positive result. We cannot create solutions for our loved ones or ourselves when we're in such a state. When we fall apart in the face of a crisis, we run the risk of perpetuating our tragic circumstances and of damaging our health, our minds, and those around us. We do not have to be victims to habitual reaction, however. We can take responsibility for our own emotional well-being. When the power to choose a productive reaction returns to us, it is a remarkable gift. We recommend the following measures as a way to begin to reclaim the power of choice during hardship:

Choose to focus on the abilities and strengths you *do* have that are beneficial. You are a resourceful, effective person. When you tell yourself otherwise, acknowledge that it is merely your pain talking. Then affirm yourself with more productive statements.

Take one day, one hour, one minute at a time when facing a crisis. Don't get ahead of yourself. In difficult circumstances, it's easy to stress about being stressed. For example, you haven't lost your job or your house, but you lie awake at night panicking about the possibilities: What will I do if we run out of money? Where will we go if we lose the house? How will we eat if I lose my job? My mother is sick; what if she dies? My son's behavior is out of control; what if he ruins his life? Indulging fears about the future, about what *might* happen, intensifies feelings of overwhelm and defeat. You don't want to be in denial about the possibilities, but obsessing about them causes you to lose sight of anything that is good in your life under the current circumstances.

Next, **acknowledge that it's difficult to recognize your strength and potential when faced with a crisis**. You may feel powerless and inadequate, as though any efforts to change the situation are like drops in the ocean.

Also, **don't focus on what you cannot do**. If you can't pay your cable bill, turn off your cable. Focus on what you can do. If you can pay your rent, rejoice in that. If the loss of certain material things is devastating for you on a physical and emotional level, accept this as an opportunity to examine your priorities, as challenging as that may be.

In my practice, I have learned that our psychology as human beings is inextricably linked to our beliefs about what is valuable and meaningful in our lives. These values are largely determined by society and culture. Many of us put our faith and security in what we have and what we can see—our jobs, our homes, and our money. "What we have" becomes equivalent to "who we are." It's no surprise that when the things we have disappear, our whole world comes crashing down.

There's nothing wrong with the American dream; working hard to have the life we want is a valuable endeavor. But if along the way, life becomes about tangible things only—the cars in the driveway, clothes in the closet, and stuff to fill our homes—we have created a false sense of security and fulfillment. This leaves us vulnerable to a crisis. If our happiness, security, and identity are determined by material, tangible things, they will vanish along with the tangibles, making a financial crisis a devastating personal event.

When our priorities in life are the intangibles—our relationships, our faith, and our integrity—we're less likely to be turned upside down by financial and material loss. When our savings are disappearing, we can choose to focus on the intangibles and be grateful for them. This is not to dismiss the pain of these losses; however, we must remember through that pain that no hardship can take away the love we have for another person or for ourselves unless we allow it. No one can take away our wisdom, our strength, or our beliefs. Nothing can take away our goals, motivation, or resilience. No crisis can take away the relationship we each have with ourselves or our relationship with God (or whatever we believe to be the underlying creative and sustaining force in the universe). These are ours forever unless we surrender them.

Times such as these give us the opportunity to discover our true selves and our true purpose in life, to look into our hearts and ask, what and who do I want to be? If we take the time to reflect on this, we can discover and seize a new purpose. The God of my understanding desires something greater for each of us than that we spend our life acquiring things that can be gone in the blink of an eye. But when the life we've built is vanishing, and it can feel that way in hard times, how do we get to a place of gratitude, peace, and renewed purpose?

When I have faced hardships in my life, and I've had a few, I review my life's priorities; I even write them down. I focus on the gifts I've been given: my health, my family, my love and compassion for others, my wisdom, and my faith and trust in God. It makes me feel inspired about the future instead of discouraged. I keep myself open to learning the new lessons life offers me. In the process of writing down my priorities, I have found that I reestablish a careful balance of tangibles and intangibles, which provides a foundation that is strong and hopeful.

Weathering the Storm

When we're facing an ongoing crisis, it can feel like we're standing outside of ourselves watching a nightmare unfold, desperately asking, "What do I do *first?*" When feeling overwhelmed in this way, we want to take very small steps to start heading in the right direction. I've included a simple list of suggestions that I hope will be helpful in keeping your heart and mind healthy as you, your friends, or your family face hard times:

Refuse to Take on the Spirit of Fear. In a crisis, fear is present on a massive level. Don't be in denial about what you're feeling. Acknowledge it, but don't let the spirit of fear overpower you. You can rise above it.

Deal with Reality. Don't hide from reality; look it straight in the eye. Look at the details of your situation, even if it is painful and scary. When you know where you stand, you can plan your next steps with all the facts on the table. There is more fear in not knowing the truth.

Recognize that Facts are Not the Complete Reality. Don't let the facts about your situation control your life. Just because you may have lost your money or your possessions doesn't mean that you've lost everything. Focus on the value of the intangibles.

Don't Let Your Emotions Dictate Your Perspective. In times such as these, emotions can be intense, but don't let them cloud your judgment. Don't let your history determine your future. Instead of fixating on what's been lost, acknowledge it and then work to shift your perspective as quickly as you can.

Appreciate What You Have. Allow yourself to appreciate the things that you do have. Also, practice focusing on the things that really matter— health, a loving family—as these are our true gifts. I find that keeping a gratitude journal is a valuable exercise in difficult times. When you start writing down the great things in your life, it's easy to see how much you have to be grateful for.

Examine Your Spiritual Life. If spirituality hasn't been a big part of your life, a crisis can really bring things into perspective. Whether you're blaming God or asking Him for help, hard times can bring spirituality into focus like never before. Seek out the spiritual mentors in your life—the church, synagogue, or wise people around you—and work toward finding the balance between trust in God's provision and taking responsibility to do your part.

Reach Out to Others. A crisis can be a lonely time, but you are not alone. You can find tremendous community and support by reaching out to others. You'll be surprised at how many families are struggling as you are; sometimes it's even harder for them. Take this opportunity to give something of yourself—whether it's resources or time—to remind yourself that you always have something to contribute, no matter what the circumstances.

Look for Opportunities. For many people, these times feel like a tragic ending. But if you choose to take the opportunity, this crisis can be an exciting new frontier. When you feel that you've lost everything, you can establish a new life any way you like. Take on a career that you've always wanted, participate differently in your relationships, and take on your own personal growth as an individual. What about your life needs to change? What possibilities could be exciting?

Find Help. If your crisis makes old wounds feel fresh and raw, you may be trying to deal with more than your present circumstances. Past pain and trauma could be hindering your ability to effectively deal with the present. Now is a great time to get the help you need. We've helped thousands of people work through their emotional burdens and pain to find relief; it can be done. You are not a lost cause.

Don't Give Up. This world still holds tremendous possibilities and will continue to turn long after your most devastating losses. Never give up on yourself. Your financial situation does not determine your worth. Crises do not last forever, and once this moment in time becomes the past, you will want to experience the great things that await you.

The final chapter in this book deals with the role of spirituality in healing trauma. Traumatic experiences can destroy trust and faith in everything and everyone, including the God we once believed in. But these experiences can also be an opening to a new and deeper sense of the divine, as many of our patients have discovered. In the process of helping to heal body and mind, we have witnessed the miraculous healing of the human spirit as well.

CHAPTER 10

The Spirituality of Healing

Trauma can seem really unfair. It inspires the age-old question: Why do bad things happen to good people? Those who work hard, obey the law, and are kind to others can still find themselves in traumatic situations. Good behavior doesn't guarantee a free pass. Even people of faith encounter difficult and painful circumstances for which there is no explanation.

This is a phenomenon that defies logic, for spiritual and nonspiritual people alike. Most of us consciously or subconsciously expect life to be fair. It doesn't make sense that a woman who desperately wants to be a mother should not be able to have children while an irresponsible teenager has two babies before her eighteenth birthday. Painful life events often seem random and undeserved. We have little control over these situations. In the darkest times, it can feel as though no one is in control and that we are at the mercy of a chaotic universe.

If we choose, we can take this chaos as evidence that God is not present in our lives. We can believe that if God existed, suffering would be reserved for those who "deserved" it, and blessings would be distributed among the "good" people. My experience has taught me that suffering is one of God's greatest gifts because it leads each of us to the God of our individual understanding. Strangely, many people who have suffered the most often look back on difficult moments with gratitude.

I have observed an essential connection between spirituality and the healing of trauma in my practice, and I am not alone. In studies, and in trauma centers around the world, psychologists and researchers from various religious, cultural, and spiritual walks have documented a predictable onset of spiritual awareness in trauma patients. One might expect that this mysterious trend would be discounted by a biochemical, physiological explanation. The connection, however, between spirituality and trauma is scientific as well as anecdotal. Many who experienced the tragedy of 9-11 in New York City have shared stories of a renewed desire to seek some kind of spiritual sustenance and restoration in an attempt to heal from the aftermath of their personal experiences.

The Physical and Emotional Nature of Spirituality

Emotions have both a spiritual and physiological aspect. They energize life, allowing you to react to your experiences. If a driver cuts you off on the freeway, you might feel angry and honk your horn. Or if your son takes out the garbage without you having to ask him, you might feel pleased. Thus, both positive and negative emotions mark our experiences, allowing us to make memories and have relationships with people we love. And the intensity of our emotions indicates our most profound experiences. The momentary sadness we feel when watching a dramatic movie pales in comparison to that of losing a loved one. The most intense emotional times often redirect the course of our lives.

Emotions are the raw materials of life experience; without them, life would be nothing more than a sequence of tasks and activities. Yet they are also the products of physiological responses. Specific areas of the brain engage so that we can feel happy, sad, scared, or joyful. We feel happy, for instance, due to activity in the left prefrontal cortex. And overactive basal ganglia can make us feel anxious and fearful. Also, neurochemicals are released as our bodies react during different emotional states. High levels of dopamine, serotonin, and norepinephrine create emotions of joy and happiness. Disrupting the flow of these substances can lead to low moods and even depression. To feel joy—or to feel loneliness—is a physical as well as an emotional experience.

We also experience spirituality through emotion and feeling. Faith inspires the deepest emotional experiences in our lives. Without the involvement of feeling, spirituality could not exist. It would be an intellectual study, and perhaps not even that! The emotion we feel when we have a life-altering, spiritual experience is very strong. The awe inspired by our experience can ignite a physical and emotional reaction powerful enough to overcome the negative emotions associated with trauma.

Many trauma victims who reach this level of healing also come to a turning point in their spiritual lives. They feel hopeful and positive about the future because they have seen the impossible become a reality. They can feel whole again, after years of feeling lost and broken. As a result, those who were without a spiritual life before their trauma can find a new beginning. Others, such as those who might have moved away from their spirituality during their time of suffering, are often reunited with their faith in a way that they hadn't known before. Healing from trauma can be a path to spiritual awakening.

Over-Spiritualizing the Healing Process

Many people find spiritual growth through a painful life experience. They might feel that they came from the darkness into the light. In the Christian community, some might say they were lost, but have now been found. It's a powerful, life-changing journey. Some trauma survivors, however, may over-spiritualize their healing process. They might adopt a rigid attitude about their newfound religious values. They may even believe that if they stay true to their faith, they will be protected from pain and suffering. All the while, they miss the opportunity to truly recover from their pain. Most distressing, many may not be experiencing genuine spiritual growth or enlightenment.

Call it misguided spirituality, counterfeit religion, or toxic faith. But inappropriate "spiritualizing" is simply another addictive behavior. Religious addiction can offer people an outlet for their pain that does not lead to long-term healing but rather creates distance between the individual and her traumatic past and the emotions that go along with it. It allows her to "check out" of her life. Be assured, however, that I don't judge religious addicts for their actions. They are, in fact, following their instinctive urges. Our instinct is to dissociate from pain. It's a defense mechanism, as when rape victims dissociate during their attack because the experience is too overwhelming for their systems to handle. Afterward, they may not remember anything about the rape itself, yet they will still be traumatized. Religious addiction is a form of dissociation, a natural human process for trauma victims. As with other addictions, however, it can hinder the healing process.

Embracing Spirituality as a Survival Mechanism

Spirituality is not just a byproduct of rehabilitation, of course. And, it's not just a survival technique. It allows us to heal and reenter the world, even after tremendous pain and suffering. It is sometimes called a blessing; it transforms our lives, giving each of us new meaning and purpose. After a traumatic experience, we need to have faith in something greater than ourselves and in a greater purpose for our lives to continue in the world without fear and to have a meaningful life. Trauma leaves its victims disengaged and disconnected from their relationships and from the world. But genuine spirituality and faith can restore that connection so that we can continue to live fully and productively, even in the face of additional trauma and suffering.

Unfortunately, no one is protected from suffering, even after reconnecting with a spiritual journey. Many people believe that if they walk in faith, they will be favored and their lives will be free of hardship. In fact, the opposite is true. People of faith often experience more pain and suffering than nonspiritual people, and no one knows this better than the Old Testament character, Job.

Job was a very faithful, righteous man. But that did not prevent him from losing everything he had, from his wealth to his family and his physical health. Job's faith was strong long before he was stripped of everything, and it continued to be strong long after his blessings were restored. He never wavered. Job refused to turn against his faith or against God. Even when he had nothing left, he held on strongly to his spirituality.

In Job's case, God used suffering as a tool to increase Job's faithfulness. Job was already a dedicated believer and remained so, even during pain. What Job went through during this time in his life is very similar to what many people are experiencing right now: he lost all of his money and belongings, suddenly and unexpectedly. Yet his faith only grew stronger. When his wealth was restored, he was not just a wealthy man. He was a wealthy man who had also suffered greatly, and he was a more complete human being as a result. He could identify with the poor as well as the rich. He could identify with the millions of other wounded people living during his time.

Trauma, once healed, can help us to identify with our fellow human beings through a shared experience. Feelings of connectedness, as opposed to isolation, can produce greater fulfillment and spiritual awareness. The idea that we are all here together points to a larger purpose. Common ground gives us the tools to come alongside one another and support each other during difficult times

In the end, Job was rewarded for his dedication, and he lived a long, abundant life. Job is an ideal human. We would all wish to remain hopeful and faithful, as Job did, during difficult times. But these things don't always happen. Sometimes it seems as though the suffering never ends. Many traumatized people wonder whether they will ever be free from their pain. There is still much to learn from Job's story about why we suffer, as humans and as people of faith, and how our lives can change for the better when we choose faith in difficult times.

Religious followers have known this for centuries and have sometimes used it as a method to develop their faith. Ascetics, those who endure suffering as an act of spiritual devotion, have existed in almost every religious tradition. They fast for weeks at a time, removed from their friends and family. They live in poverty and enforced silence. Some extreme ascetics have endured physical pain, through whipping or branding, in the name of God.

For these men and women, their times of suffering were the most spiritually rewarding moments of their lives. They felt closer to God and chose to develop their spirituality through self-inflicted pain. I don't believe it's necessary to go to this extreme. Real-life suffering and sacrifice are all around us, and they find us whether we want them to do so or not.

Most traumatized people didn't choose their experiences. They would do almost anything to erase these events from their history. Some soldiers wish they had never gone to war. Some children wish they had been born to different parents. They look at people around them and wonder, "Why did this happen to *me*?" It can be very difficult to see the good in any traumatic experience. In the midst of pain, we can't see the forest for the trees.

Why does God allow these things to happen to innocent people? Are we all being punished? Humans have grappled with these questions for ages. I don't pretend to understand all the workings of the universe, but I do believe God brings light to a dark situation. I also believe that He doesn't interfere with our ability to choose what we do, how we live, or what we believe in. As a result, we make mistakes. We hurt each other. And after thousands of years of the human decision-making process, we have created a flawed world full of flawed people. The results aren't perfect, but without the gift of choice, life wouldn't be the amazing journey that it is.

More importantly, I believe God is "there" for us when we falter to help us get back up again. I don't believe that God sets us up to fail, even though He knows we will. It's inevitable that we will fail; we are human, after all. Rather than setting us up for failure, He allows us to heal from our mistakes. He even makes it possible for us to heal from the mistakes of others so we can have meaningful, spirit-altering experiences in a world that, at times, seems hopeless.

Looking around at the chaotic world, it is sometimes difficult to see God. But if we know what we are looking for, we will realize that God is everywhere. Through our suffering, we have the opportunity to grow. Pain, in the form of trauma, can teach us to believe in things we never thought possible, and our ability to heal from suffering is nothing short of a miracle. When I have the opportunity to watch someone change in front of my eyes, I know that I'm witnessing God's work. These survivors of trauma are completely transformed, becoming more authentic versions of themselves.

Spirituality is essential to human life. A spiritual journey helps us to develop the tools, attitudes, and emotions that foster the healing process. It equips us to face past trauma and to heal its ravages; it gives us strength without the need to *armor* ourselves to the detriment of our minds and bodies. A deep faith can be a healthy defense against the woes of the world, making each of us feel stronger, more capable and connected, which in turn makes the world a better place.

Acknowledgments

With the publication of *Trauma: Healing the Hidden Epidemic*, I welcome the opportunity to share my personal and professional thoughts, experiences, and skills. The process of recording on paper the significant changes that have occurred to me up to this point in my life and career has been both challenging and satisfying.

I live my life and carry out my work with a day-by-day commitment to helping people through the darkest hours of their lives. I strive to give them hope and encouragement, using my clinical skills to help them heal. It has been my job and my privilege for over forty years to also help my patients find purpose in their suffering and pain. Wise counsel has certainly been an important component in this healing process. However, I discovered many years ago that words alone are not enough; without understanding the body and its vast and complex impact on the mind, the unconscious, and on our behaviors, habits, and reactions, there can be no real healing. Discovering new ways to provide real healing has been and continues to be my life's work.

I want to acknowledge someone who is probably one of the greatest minds of the twentieth century in this pursuit: Dr. Wilhelm Reich. Dr. Reich was brilliant in his insights into psychoanalysis and was a man who continually thought and worked "outside the box."

Since Reich's time, there have been many refinements and improvements to his work. I believe our practice at the Bernstein Institute for Trauma Treatment has contributed to this refinement, taking Reichian psychotherapeutic clinical effectiveness to a new level. Foundational contributions to our work have come from other sources as well. As in so many other disciplines, we have built on the shoulders of many great thinkers, practitioners, mentors, and assistants.

First and foremost, I want to thank my wife, Lynn, who for the past thirty-eight years has been the greatest source of inspiration to my life and to the development of my work. Thank you, Lynn, my beloved and true partner. Without you, none of this would have happened.

Next, I want to thank several mentors whose help, wisdom, and encouragement have made it possible for me to be here today, finishing this book.

I want to express my most profound gratitude to the late Dr. Gerald Frank, D.C. Without his help, I would not be the psychotherapist I have become, and I could not have developed such a deep understanding of the body, mind, and spirit connection without him.

I also want to thank a true friend, Mr. Armando Maliano, whose wisdom, "street-wise" experience, and knowledge of the alcohol-drug addiction syndrome have made me a more adept and sensitive therapist. His steadfast guidance has enabled me to comprehend the deep and destructive connections between addiction, trauma, and the body and to work in the addiction field without judgment or condemnation. He has been a wonderful partner in understanding and treating family systems in new and innovative ways. Thanks, Mando.

My long path of personal growth has taken me through some traumatic life experiences. Eventually, I needed to go through my own spiritual "overhaul." I want to thank Pastor Ken Gage and his inspiring wife, Joy—an author in her own right—who mentored me in years past. It was Joy's encouragement to write this book that stirred my vision. Thank you, Ken and Joy; I have been blessed by both of you.

There is another very special person who has long been looking forward to the completion of this book: my mother, Pauline. We have had our ups and downs, but she is now one of the strongest voices of wisdom, love, strength, and support in my life.

I want to explain that my mother may have trouble reading some of my traumatic history because long ago she was involved in it. But my mother and I have forever healed our traumatic relationship and reconciled. Today she is an amazing mother and friend who is at my side whenever I need her. As I tell her, "It is never too late to heal, forgive, and reconcile, God willing." Thank you, Mom.

Additionally, I want to thank several amazing assistants on my clinical staff.

First, there is Mrs. Jennifer Stevenson, my stalwart and brilliant administrative assistant. Formerly a chemical engineer by profession, she now calls herself an "engineer in recovery." Her talents and gifts have grown, and she has "morphed" into an astounding team member, coach, bodyworker, administrator, writer, and all-around inspiration to me and to others.

I also want to thank the beautiful and gracious Mrs. Hilloah Levy, who at an advanced age made the decision to develop into a team practitioner, coach, bodyworker, writer, designer, and incredible gardener at our institute. She states that she went from being self-involved and selfish to being a selfless and uncomplaining giver. Hilloah shares her many gifts every day.

My deepest gratitude also goes to Katherine Dieter for her many hours of refining and reorganizing our manuscript. She has worked sensitively and conscientiously with our team during many rewrites and corrections of our book.

I also want to thank Stephen Rustad for his outstanding design work and numerous other creative contributions. Steve's passion for helping to shape and communicate my message of hope and healing has never wavered.

I also want to thank Kate Long Hollingsworth for her assistance in helping us with the original rough draft of this book.

Her willingness to stretch herself and to grow and learn as she read and worked with us on the original manuscript has been much appreciated.

I don't want to forget for a moment the brilliant contributions that Mr. John Barnes, P.T. has made to the field of myofascial release physical therapy. Through him, I learned many of the skills that I have experimented with and incorporated into my practice as I created Reichian-Myofascial Release Therapy (RMFR). John taught me sensitivity to the subtleties of working with the body that I never knew before.

There are many others who have contributed to the creation of our new modality for treating pain—physical, emotional, psychological, and spiritual. Our work continues, with new treatment forms combining bodywork and psychotherapy in development. May this work continue long after I'm gone, and may the creative process also continue so that new, even more effective ways to relieve pain, trauma, and suffering will be found. It is to the "joy in the morning" that my life's work is committed.

Bibliography

Arterburn, Stephen, and Jack Felton. *Toxic Faith: Understanding & Overcoming Religious Addiction*. Nashville, TN: Oliver-Nelson Books, 1991.

Baker, Elsworth F. *Man in the Trap: The Causes of Blocked Sexual Energy*. New York: The Macmillan Publishing Company, Inc., 1967.

Barnes, John F. *Healing Ancient Wounds: The Renegades Wisdom*. Paoli, Pennsylvania: Rehabilitation Services, Inc., T/A, 2000.

Barnes, John F. *Myofascial Release: The Search for Excellence*. Paoli, Pennsylvania: Rehabilitation Services, Inc., T/A, 1990.

Boadella, David. *Wilhelm Reich: The Evolution of his Work*. New York: Dell Publishing Co., Inc., 1973.

Fair, David. Advisor for the National Center for Crisis Management. Brownwood, Texas [or Ronkonkoma, New York]

Gellhorn, Ernst. *Autonomic Imbalance and the Hypothalamus: Implications for Physiology, Medicine, Psychology, and Neuropsychiatry*. Minneapolis: University of Minnesota Press, 1957.

Greene, Elliot, and Barbara Goodrich-Dunn. *The Psychology of the Body (LWW Massage Therapy and Bodywork Educational Series)*. Baltimore: Lippincott Williams & Wilkins, 2004.

Henslin, Earl, and Daniel Amen. *This is Your Brain on Joy: A Revolutionary Program for Balancing Mind, Restoring*

Brain Health, and Nurturing Spiritual Growth. Nashville: Thomas Nelson, 2009.

Levine, Peter. *Waking the Tiger: Healing Trauma*. Berkeley: North Atlantic Books, 1997.

Mitchell, Jeffrey T. *Critical Incident Stress Management (CISM): Group Crisis Intervention, 4th Edition*. Elliott City, Maryland: International Critical Incident Stress Foundation, Inc., 2006.

Reich, Wilhelm. *Early Writings, Volume One*. Translated by Philip Schmitz. New York: Farrar, Straus and Giroux, 1975.

Reich, Wilhelm. *Character Analysis*. Translated by Vincent R. Carfagno. New York: Simon and Schuster, 1972.

Selye, Hans. *The Stress of Life*. Revised edition. New York: McGraw-Hill Book Company, 1976.

Tanielian, Terri, and Lisa H Jaycox, Editors. *Invisible Wounds of War: Psychological and Cognitive Injuries, Their Consequences, and Services to Assist Recovery*. Santa Monica: Rand Corporation, 2008.

About Dr. Bernstein

Peter M. Bernstein received his master's in Social Psychology, Department of Sociology, from San Jose State University and his doctorate in Clinical Psychology from International University. He completed a professional certification program in Reichian therapy with Gerald Frank, DC, and received post-doctoral recognition from the American Psychotherapy Association as a Diplomate and Fellow. Formerly the Clinical Director of Center Point Drug and Alcohol Treatment Programs, Dr. Bernstein has been in private practice since 1974 as a licensed Marriage and Family Therapist and is the founder and director of the Bernstein Institute for Integrative Psychotherapy and Trauma Treatment. He is the creator of Reichian Myofascial Release Therapy (RMFR), a new modality to treat physical and emotional pain and trauma.

Dr. Bernstein is the author of numerous published articles and has led a wide variety of workshops for professionals, including resiliency and secondary trauma training for case workers and clinical staff at the Department of Veterans Affairs. He helped found and continues to be the moving force behind Sonoma Coast Trauma Treatment, a non-profit foundation dedicated to healing combat-related trauma for veterans, service members and their families.

An Army infantry veteran of the Vietnam War era, Dr. Bernstein and his wife, Lynn, live in Petaluma, California. He can be contacted at www.bernsteininstitute.com.

Made in the USA
Lexington, KY
17 June 2015